Architecting EU Solutions

Brian Suhr

Copyright © 2016 by Brian Suhr.

All rights reserved. No part of this publication may be reproduced, distributed or transmitted in any form or by any means, including photocopying, recording, or other electronic or mechanical methods, without the prior written permission of the publisher, except in the case of brief quotations embodied in critical reviews and certain other noncommercial uses permitted by copyright law. For permission requests, write to the publisher at the email address below.

Brian Suhr
www.virtualizetips.com
brian@virtualizetips.com

Ordering Information:
Quantity sales. Special discounts are available on quantity purchases by corporations, associations, and others. For details, contact the publisher at the address above.

Architecting EUC Solutions/ Brian Suhr. —1st edition
ISBN 978-1530879342

Contents

Developing Your Strategy and Roadmap 1
    Developing your requirements 2
    What Services Will You Provide? 5
    Marketing Your EUC Services 5
    Selecting An EUC Vendor 7
    Building Your EUC Roadmap 9

Use Cases 13
    How to identify use cases 14
    Use case attributes 16
    Finding Common Ground 18
    Summary 21

Starting the Design Process 23
    Project Requirements 24
    Revisit Use Case Requirements 25
    Design Layers 27
    Conceptual Layer 29
    Logical Layer 30
    Physical Layer 31
    Summary 33

Pilots and Proof of Concepts 35
    Proof of Concepts 35
    Externally Driven POC 39

Pilots 39

Summary 41

Desktop Assessments 43

What are the Options? 43

Assessment Tools 44

How Long Does the Process Take? 45

What Do You Want to Discover? 47

Application Discovery 50

Summary 52

Virtual Desktops 53

How Virtualization Helps 54

Desktop Types 54

Persistent Desktops 55

Non-Persistent Desktops 59

Use Cases – Non-Persistent Desktops 67

Dedicated vs. Pooled Non-Persistent Desktops 68

Shared Hosted Desktops 68

3D Graphics Accelerations 70

Summary 72

Physical PCs and Laptops 73

The Challenge 74

The Desired State 75

Rich Endpoints 77

Power Users 77

Bring Your Own Device 78

Offline Use Cases.. 79

Summary 80

Desktop as a Service 81

DaaS Pros.. 82

DaaS Cons... 84

DaaS Questions 85

Use Cases 87

Summary 88

Application Management.. 91

Why is it Called Application Management? 92

Application Management Alternatives 99

Natively Installed 100

Application Presentation 103

Application Layering 106

Applications Virtualization 109

User Installed Applications 112

Summary 113

User Profiles... 115

Profile Management Options 116

Features to consider 118

Things to Watch Out For 120

Risks of Folder Redirection 121

Disaster Recovery 122

Summary 124

Portal 125

Entitlement 125

Single Sign On 126

Enterprise App Store 127

Customization 130

Summary 130

Disaster Recovery 133

Vendor Architectures 134

DR Capacity 135

Disaster Recovery Alternatives 135

Active / Cold 136

Active / Warm 139

Active / Active 141

Cloud services 144

Do You Still Need Backups? 145

Summary 146

Networking 147

How Many Networks Will You Need? 147

Network Monitoring 150

What are Your DHCP Needs? 151

Network Latency 152

Network Bandwidth 154

Data Center View 155

- Remote Connection View 156
- Remote Office View 156
- Load Balancing 158
- Network Firewalls 159
- Summary 159

Operations 161
- Reporting 161
- Monitoring 164
- Operational Items 165
- EUC Team 166
- Team Building 170
- Summary 174

Infrastructure 175
- Entry Point 176
- Scalability 177
- Performance 178
- Capacity 179
- Monitoring 180
- Building Blocks 181
- Infrastructure Alternatives 183
- Storage Requirements 190
- Storage Types 193
- Compute Sizing 195
- vSphere Cluster Design 198

v

Summary	200
Security	201
User Access	202
Two-factor authentication	203
Data Access Policies	204
Antivirus	205
SSL Certificates	207
Audits	208
Access Path	209
Network Isolation and Segmentation	209
Micro Segmentation	212
Summary	214
Endpoints	215
Endpoint types	216
Why Do They Matter?	217
Evaluating thin clients	221
Decision tree sample	222
Summary	223
Appendix – Nutanix Design Example	225
Single vCPU Desktops	227
Dual vCPU Desktops	229
Management Cluster	230
Nutanix Storage Cluster Alternatives	231
Summary	235

Index..236

Dedication

To my wife Nicholle and our kids for their support and patience during the book writing process, allowing me to spend all the hours that I spent stuck in front of a computer.
Brian Suhr

Foreword

I am humbled to write a foreword for Brian's End-User Computing (EUC) book. Five years ago in 2010-11, Nutanix was looking for a "killer app" for its new web-scale infrastructure. Like most well-designed companies, we were unwilling to spray-n-pray our bold architecture on any and every workload. After all, every large company started small, with a single workload, a single audience -- and that provided focus, a necessary attention to detail that keeps ambitious companies grounded. Rather than be all things to all people, Microsoft early on focused on productivity apps for the office professional. VMware, similarly, focused on test-n-dev as its killer app. So did NetApp and AWS. They finessed their products with their respective killer apps, built an honest ecosystem on the strong foundation of customer delight, and very successfully mined their own exhaust, pumping profits back to build a much broader product portfolio for a larger audience. That iterative business design is at the core of iconic long-lasting companies.

For Nutanix, that killer app was EUC. At the core of EUC is building a cloud infrastructure for virtual desktops, popularly called VDI. Our early advisors warned us that VDI was a high-risk application. It was extremely mission-critical for the enterprise front-office, much more than a back-office business software traditionally seen as the workhorse of any enterprise business. Think about it. A desktop is so fundamental that, if unavailable, can bring down an entire business, with no access to a browser -- Internet, SaaS apps, social networks (!) -- let alone access to back-office applications. When Nutanix was forming, VDI was considered "dead on arrival" by most industry watchers, including media pundits, analysts, VCs, and disappointed CIOs who saw their budgets bleed and their end users seethe. It had classically flattered to deceive, and had amassed an entire army of detractors who balked at its poor user experience and unsustainable economics.

A desktop in 2010 was considered a commodity. Aggregating thousands of these commodity units into a cloud was an obvious next step, especially because:

- IOS and Android were coming to the edge, so Windows had to end up in the cloud,
- end users wanted universal access to their desktop environment, and
- security breaches in a truly interconnected world meant that data needed to come "within the perimeter," rather than being scattered under thousands of desks.

VDI was an embarrassingly parallel workload, and a perfect match for a distributed system architecture. Unfortunately, legacy vendors were trying to fit a square peg in a round hole by forcing a dual-controller 3-tier datacenter architecture onto an eminently parallel workload. Moreover, VDI needed to start small, like most well-behaved clouds -- allowing for the infrastructure to grow over time. But legacy infrastructure vendors were selling large monolithic pods to customers, bringing a bad name to VDI, because the unit economics at small numbers was simply vulgar!

Nutanix looked at that disillusionment as a massive opportunity. We took a big risk in embracing a highly mission-critical workload as our killer app, our 1st workload. It helped build a beautiful empathy-driven company -- an honest product and an honest customer service. We focused intensely on product reliability, usability, and availability, much more than most Silicon Valley startups enamored by speeds-n-feeds. We built the best enterprise customer support team in contemporary times because an unavailable desktop was a blemish on the company's aspirations to become an invisible infrastructure for the enterprise. VDI drove us to do impossible things. And while today, it is less than 1/3rd of our business, it is still the workload that keeps us grounded.

I am proud to see one of our own employees, Brian Suhr, write a treatise on EUC. I've followed his work well before he started at Nutanix, when he was still at Ahead. I've personally spent time trying to hire Brian, and continue to work with him on understanding the IT landscape around us. With his broader focus on EUC, he attempts to look at the bigger picture of consumerization in the enterprise. He has worked the whole body looking at security, networking, applications, and business continuity facets of end user computing. You will enjoy reading something this holistic.

Dheeraj Pandey, CEO & Founder, Nutanix

About the Authors

Brian Suhr is a Senior Technical Marketing Engineer on the Product and Technical Marketing team at Nutanix, Inc. Prior to his Nutanix role Brian worked as a Solutions Architect for a consulting organization for a number of years. Overall Brian has worked in IT for over twenty years in consulting, architecture and engineering roles. A strong background in server and desktop virtualization has given him the opportunity to work with many different applications and architectures. Brian is a VMware Certified Design Expert (VCDX #118), has written extensively on personal and industry blog sites, and has been a speaker at multiple public and private events. He can be followed @bsuhr

Contributions by:
Sean Massey has been working in the field of IT for 10 years. He is a consultant focusing on the virtual End User Computing and Mobility space for AHEAD. He is a semi-active blogger at http://thevirtualhorizon.com and is a VMware EUC Champion, Nutanix Technology Champion, and Pernix Pro. He currently lives in Kimberly, WI, with his wife, Laura, and their two children and two cats. He can be followed @seanpmassey

About the Reviewers

Kees Baggerman – Kees is a senior solution architect for End-User Computing at Nutanix Inc. In his role, Kees develops methods for successfully implementing applications on the Nutanix platform. In addition, he delivers customer projects, including defining architectural, business, and technical requirements, creating designs, and implementing the Nutanix solution.

Before working with Nutanix, Kees' main areas of work were migrations and implementations of Microsoft and Citrix infrastructures, writing functional/technical designs for Microsoft infrastructures, Microsoft Terminal Server or Citrix (Presentation Server/ XenApp, XenDesktop and NetScaler) in combination with RES Workspace Manager, and RES Automation Manager.

Kees is a Citrix Certified Integration Architect, Microsoft Certified IT Professional, RES Certified Professional, and RES Certified Trainer. RES Software also named him RES RSVP six consecutive years, and Kees was honored as the RES Software Most Valuable Professional of 2011. As a demonstration of his passion for virtualization technology, Kees earned the title of VMware vExpert in 2013, 2014, and 2015. Citrix also named him a Citrix Technology Professional in 2015.

Acknowledgments

The opinions expressed in this book are the authors' personal opinions and based on personal experience. Statements made throughout this book do not reflect the views and opinions of any vendor mentioned.

I would like to thank my old consulting team at AHEAD for some great experiences on different projects and the opportunity to learn and grow with some smart people. In particular, I would like to call out a few individuals, Sean Massey, Kees Baggerman, and Thomas Brown. These guys have been great at helping and providing feedback over the years.

I must also give credit to my wife Nicholle for the help in selecting a cover design and not allowing me to mess that part of the process up.

Brian Suhr

Introduction

In many organizations there are server teams: network teams, storage teams, and desktop teams. These teams operate as silos, and only share server virtualization as a commonality. There does not seem to be many End-User Computing (EUC) teams yet. This, though, is changing, as organizations look for ways to deal with the demand for modern end-user services. The fact of the matter is that EUC will touch each of the individual components and teams in its attempt to offer the best possible end-user experience.

Since smartphones have become standard, and employees demand to have choice in their endpoints, organizations have been forced to deal with these disruptive trends. End users are increasingly mobile and want choice in the devices that they use. Gone are the days when organizations can hand out the standard black laptop, and expect everyone to be happy. Now organizations are offering a variety of options in their device offerings (CYOD) or allowing employees to bring their own device (BYOD).

The motivation of this book is to not sell you on the idea of modern EUC, but rather arm you with details needed to tackle many of these disruptive items. The book is not a step-by-step how to install VMware Horizon, or answer what are the resource requirements for XenApp serves with a specific user density.

What the book does offer is architecture guidance for building a strategy, design, and roadmap for a modern EUC environment. The book will help answer questions as you move through these phases, and educate you on questions you should be asking during them. It is intended to be helpful whether you are in an architecture role internally or on the partner/vendor side.

The book intentionally does not focus on any specific offering from a particular vendor. Different chapters will provide insight and guidance on the different aspects of EUC services and what topics should be covered.

These details and questions will help you in your EUC projects. Whether you are evaluating products and vendors or have a project to design a solution, you will be better prepared for success after reading this book.

Introduction to EUC

Before getting too deep into the book, an explanation of what makes up a modern EUC environment is in order. It is becoming accepted that a modern EUC environment is made up of multiple services. These services are listed in the diagram below:

EUC Services

- Mobile Management
- Application Management
- Virtual & Physical Desktops
- Centralized Portal Authentication
- User Persona and Files
- Operations Management

Virtual Desktops (VDI/SBC)

Virtual Desktops (VDI) and Server-Based Computing (SBC) will likely not be anything new to anyone reading this book. There are different methods for providing a centralized desktop. Organizations can use VDI by providing a separate instance of an OS to each user or use a hosted shared desktop (SBC) method that allows a group of users to share a server OS, and still get an individual desktop experience. Additionally, in some edge use cases, organizations may have a need to present a physical PC or server to users virtually to allow them to consume the full resources of a dedicated device.

Physical PCs and Laptops

Even with very cool and powerful mobile devices, there is still a large number of physical devices being used by organizations today. The usage ranges from using existing endpoints as your access point into a virtual desktop, perhaps for use cases that require the power of a physical device, or maybe the mobility of a laptop when disconnected. The reality is that for most organizations it will be impossible to believe that you can provide 100% of your desktop based use cases with virtual desktops.

Understanding that there are a variety of use cases, organizations will need to determine which of their use cases would require or benefit from using a full featured physical device. Details about how to identify use cases and gather requirements will be covered in Chapter 2. The focus on utilizing physical devices in your design should be about meeting requirements and improving the operational management for these devices. These points should be addressed with a fresh perspective instead of what has been done historically within your organization.

Application Management

"Applications are King" is the mantra that you should live by. Users typically do not come begging to get access to a Windows desktop. The applications and data are what your users need to perform their work each day; it is how they enter/analyze data, make sales, assist customers, etc. This means that application access is imperative to doing business, whether they are locally installed or abstracted in some manner. An increasing number of organizations demand access to applications from multiple devices, or even any type of device. This means that the users do not want to be tied to a specific PC in an office to use a certain application. They would like to use any application from their work PC, personal laptop, or maybe a mobile tablet.

The ability to provide flexibility in your ability to manage, update, and present your organization's applications is going to be a critical piece of your design. As you gather requirements from the use cases, you will be evaluating how each application should be presented and managed. The architecture team will then select the application management options that will be able to provide the flexibility to meet the requirements of the use cases. Chapter 9 will be covering application management in detail to prepare you for these decisions.

User Persona

Having a consistent and personal experience with the EUC services is what your end users will expect. If you do not provide this, you will have trouble with adoption, and user satisfaction will be low. To provide a consistent experience and with supported user personalization, you will need to capture and manage each user's persona. This is also commonly referred to as the user's profile, and is quickly evolving to User Environment Management (UEM). The user profile is part of what UEM offers, but it also includes application settings, as well as policies and settings. As EUC services become less dependent on a desktop OS, the user's persona will become managing more than just OS variables over time.

This approach will allow users to customize their personal experience within approved guidelines. Each user can then enjoy the picture of his dog as their background, have her customized application settings, dictionary and other settings persist. Chapter 10 will detail the design consideration around user personas.

User Files

After applications, user's files are the most important part of the EUC landscape. Some use cases will include users that create large amount of data, while others will create little to no unique data. These user files are office documents, PDFs, pictures, media, and any of the other hundreds of potential file types that users consume. They will be creating, editing and sharing these files, and they will want this to be seamless.

There are a number of ways to design a solution to meet these requirements, many are flawed. The leading approach to this is commonly referred to as Enterprise File Sync and Share (EFSS). This is simply providing a Dropbox-like experience to your users, while the organizations still own the data and controls policy. The EFSS type of services allows users to access data on multiple devices and supports secure sharing while enabling the organization to have visibility and control around the service.

Mobile Management

Last time anyone walked through the average workplace, mobile devices are not on the decline. They are like a zombie virus spreading with extreme prejudice and no signs of slowing down. Users have become addicted to using mobile devices in their personal lives, and they are calling for a similar experience in the workplace. Some organizations began experimenting with this by allowing a small number of users to access data without restrictions or management as a method to appease them. This typically grows, and then you end up with hundreds of unmanaged devices accessing applications and data.

The demand is real, as is the risk for organizations. Having a properly architected strategy and design around the use and access of mobile devices is critical. There are a number of ways to accomplish this and within your organization you may even need to take more than one approach. The leading methods for this have been by managing the device (Mobile Device Management) or the apps (Mobile Application Management) and data (Mobile Information Management) on a device.

Operations Management

In the past, operations teams have had little insight into what was going on with individual desktops; there was not much need for it. If there was an issue, they would go investigate and maybe run Perfmon on the Windows desktop. With adoption of virtualized and centralized EUC services, the need to improve the operational story and visibility must be a founding principal of your design. You are going to be abstracting services from individual's endpoints in many cases, and you will need to understand performance, capacity planning, security and other aspects. Evaluating and selecting monitoring and reporting tool(s) must be accounted for in your design. Later in Chapter 14 the operational needs will be discussed in detail.

Centralized Portal

A centralized portal can serve as a single point of entry to an organization's EUC services. This portal is often referred to as an enterprise app store. The portal can also server as your Single-Sign-On (SSO) point, allowing one login before accessing the individual services. This might be the most attractive feature of these portals.

Other than authentication, users will see all of their services from a single web page. Allowing them, with a touch or mouse click, to launch an application or desktop. On the operations side, this can have benefits also because there is increasingly a single place to entitle and un-entitle users to these services.

Allowing you to easily turn users on or off without visiting multiple element managers. The portal subject will be covered in more detail in Chapter 11.

Along with these services, there are supporting and common infrastructure services, as well as the infrastructure required for these to run upon. All of these services will be touched upon within the chapters of the book. The infrastructure to run these services on will also be covered later in Chapter 15.

Major EUC Players

If you are evaluating vendors, there are just a few that offer a complete or near complete solution for this modern EUC approach. This book does not intend to sway you in any direction. There is a lot of value to vendors that offer these EUC services in a licensing suite, as it affords the customer access to more of these services than the previous death by a thousand licenses.

It is becoming common belief that customers will, for the most part, receive a better-integrated solution by adopting the suite from a vendor of your choice. The opportunity to fully integrate these services by each vendor is already happening by them and will continue to mature over the next year or two.

The following are the vendors that are felt to have the most complete offerings, and can either fulfill all of the services outlined earlier or a significant amount of them.

- Citrix
- VMware
- Microsoft
- Dell

[1]

Developing Your Strategy and Roadmap

What is your strategy? The definition of a strategy is "a plan of action or policy designed to achieve a major or overall aim". Simply put, you have to figure out where you are going and why, to know how to get their and then be able to quantify if you were successful.

Without a proper EUC strategy, organizations will struggle to define what they want to provide versus, what they need to provide to their end users. Having a strategy is a necessity, unless you are just going to provide one service, such as VDI, and have already picked your vendor, though it is still likely that a strategy is needed even in that scenario. Questions to ask could include? How will you deal with applications in the VDI environment versus the physical desktop environment for example? Maybe you will just do the same or use a different method, which is right?

There will be some organizations that say they need to offer desktops, and they just want a design. This is when you should push back, and recommend a strategy phase. Not everyone will approach things in the same manner, and you will have mixed reactions. This book is not a business plan approach for building your EUC strategy, only your organization can establish that. It will prepare you with information to feed these discussions and hopefully make it clear why a strategy is important.

The chapters of this book were created to educate organizations on EUC services, and things for which they should be preparing and asking. These will aide in developing your strategy and design for EUC services.

Developing your requirements

As part of any properly run project, you will need to develop what the requirements are. This is important whether you are in the strategy or design phase. Ideally, you should start in the strategy phase and identify the requirements and adjust them if necessary in the design phase of the project.

As part of the requirements phase of your project, you need to identify your Objectives, Constraints, Risks, and Assumptions. These will help you in your strategy and design journey. This process should just not be a discussion among a few engineers and architects in the IT organization.

To have a successfully EUC project there must be management involvement from the IT and business sides of the organization. These leaders will be necessary to drive the transition these services will bring, as well as have enough power to drive the adoption. They can also act as a communication point to request business needs and do a validation of the technical translation. The following is a short description of these terms:

- **Objectives** - Objectives are the reasons why the project has been initiated. A project's outcomes may be the products or services you develop or the results of using these products and services.
- **Constraints** – Constrains are factors that you will need to consider during the life of the project that you cannot change. These may include deadlines, regulatory requirements, technology decisions and dependencies on other projects to deliver.

- **Risks** - There may be potential external events that will have a negative impact on your project if they occur. Risk refers to the combined likelihood the event will occur and the impact on the project if the event does occur. If the combined likelihood of the event happening and impact to the project are both high, you should identify the potential event as a risk and put a plan in place to manage it.
- **Assumptions** - Within a project there are going to be details that will not be available or are out of your control. You will need to accept them as fact or as certain to happen, without proof. These will be considered assumptions in your project. They will need to be called out and published to your project team, and when possible referenced in documentation when applicable.

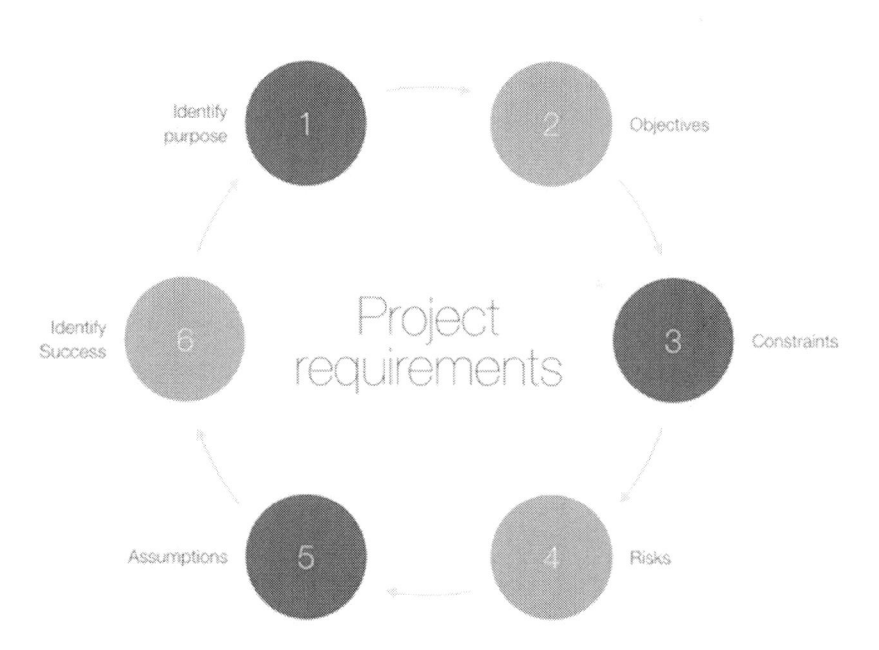

Diagram: Circular flow of Project requirements — 1. Identify purpose, 2. Objectives, 3. Constraints, 4. Risks, 5. Assumptions, 6. Identify Success

Just for a small sample a few Objectives, Constraints, Risks, and Assumptions are listed below. These are not meant to be used without validation or as an exhaustive for your EUC project, but rather just provide an idea of what they might look like.

Objectives
- Improve operation efficiency
- Allow for company owned devices and BYOD
- Simplify remote access
- Enable role based application access
- Simplify frequent application updates
- Extend life of existing endpoints
- Improve desktop management

Constraints
- Improve usability without reducing security
- Limited resources for implementation
- Must utilize storage from specific vendor

Risks
- Project funding is limited
- Must utilize existing storage array
- Current staff has little EUC experience
- Data center space might not be ready

Assumptions
- The new data center space will be acquired and prepared in time for deployment
- The organization or your customer will hire resources to meet deadlines
- New EUC team will be created
- New infrastructure is deployed and ready
- Deployment will only include documented use cases and services

What Services Will You Provide?

In developing your EUC strategy a list of services will need to be assembled. This list is not set in stone, but will be used as your project moves forward. Changes to the list can have a negative effect on the project outcome. Ideally you are trying to develop your strategy as a vision for the next several years, not just a short-term view because of an immediate need.

The list of services can be taken from the list that was provided in the Introduction section earlier. Your organization's strategy may use some, all, or even ones not contained in the list earlier in this chapter. It is important to precisely define them in your strategy.

When researching which services you will include as part of your strategy, you should include services that are heavily driven by your project's requirements. If you have worked with the business, they will have or will provide you with their requirements and requests. It is your duty as a leader or architect to ultimately decide if you can fulfill all the requests or narrow it to a subset, and communicate this back to the business and project team.

> *A piece of advice is to pay attention to the real business needs, and do not spend your time trying to find targets to use on which you can experiment with this cool technology.*

If you take the approach of trying to find a target problem, and then try to solve it with EUC services, you will not have the best results. There are generally enough concrete business needs to build your strategy around and make sure you validate your interpretations with the business.

Marketing Your EUC Services

Something that internal IT has done a historically bad job about is marketing what they have to offer the business. For a long time IT has been a black box that most business users under value or cannot fully explain what is there for. IT needs to stop being a line item on a profit and loss sheet and bring value to the business.

A major way that you can add value to the business is through offering the types of EUC services that are being discussed in this book. If, however, you do a bad job at letting your users know what is available, it will not do much good. You can guarantee that Amazon, VMware, Citrix, and other Cloud services are doing a good job at marketing what services they have to offer, and are enticing users to head on over and swipe their credit card or download an app and start consuming them.

This is where IT could benefit by hiring a marketing person to be part of their team. Make no mistake, you are in a fight with external services for the attention and business of your users. The marketing and communication of what you are building around your EUC services is just as important as many design aspects.

You need to inform the business leaders and users about what services you can offer them around mobility, desktops, file services, and working remotely. You do not want to build it, and have no one show up. "Because we build it, they will come" does not hold true when it comes to these types of modern services that can be acquired from multiple sources.

How you inform business users is something that will need to be cultivated internally. You can use the corporate communications team for some messaging, meet with specific leaders to educate and ask them to help market the services, hold some type of town hall or brownbag type of meetings, and look at using other forms of communication available internally. If all else fails work up some type of catchy retro marketing poster and place strategically through the campus.

Selecting an EUC Vendor

In the strategy phase, you will be working towards your vendor selection. You may start out with a vendor selected already, but ideally you are building your strategy with an open mind. Then, towards the end of your strategy development, you are ready to make your vendor choice. This process should have helped you in your evaluation of the different vendor offerings and made the decision easier.

Picking the right vendor to fulfill your EUC vision will not be an easy choice. By using the guidance of this book you will be better educated to make this decision. It may be a close process and just come down to a financial decision based on which vendor wants your business more. Typically, most organizations have some sort of formalized vendor or solution based evaluation and decision process. If not, there is maybe something that is used, though it may not be a finally tuned process within the teams.

Once selected, the organization will be committed to the vendor and solution for a couple of years at minimum. It is highly recommended to continue to follow the advances of the vendor chosen as well as the alternatives not selected. This can be done on a yearly basis or when major new versions are released, allowing the architect to ensure that there is not a compelling reason to re-evaluate options again.

An approach that you can consider, modify or add to your existing evaluation process is to use some sort of a weighted scoring system or score card. In this approach you would use your identified requirements, objectives, and list of EUC services you want to provide. These would be the data points that you would use and research whether each vendor can accommodate these data points and possibly how well they can.

The diagram below is using the numbered boxes to represent the data points that matter to the organization. If each vendor is able to meet or accommodate the data point it is moved into their respective box. If a vendor is able to do a better job at that data point a different color or higher value is applied to it. Any data points that cannot be accommodated by any of the vendors should be left unassigned.

The diagram below is a visually simple way to illustrate this idea. You can also consider using more of a table based approach that uses a weighted number scoring system. Then the vendor with the highest score is your likely choice. The point here is to offer guidance to work towards a decision and not that you must use a specific format.

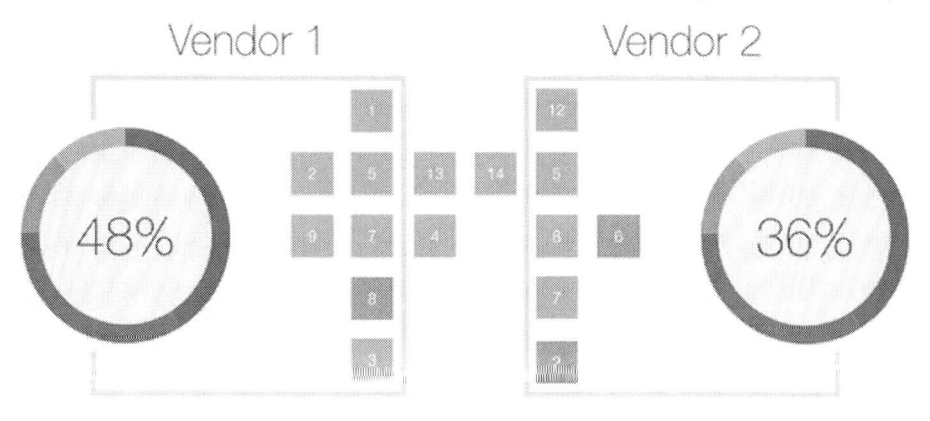

A few other things to consider in your selection process, is there a vendor that offers a more complete solution in regards to your requirements? Do you have a particularly difficult use case that one vendor can address while still providing a leading solution for your other use cases?

To assist with evaluating the vendors and product features, most organizations might build a small test environment just to familiarize themselves with how the products function. If you look at more than one vendor in this process it might be referred to as a bake off. Do not confuse this with a pilot or proof of concept; those will be covered in detail in Chapter 4.

Building Your EUC Roadmap

Another important part of your EUC journey is developing a roadmap for the solution that you will ultimately design and build. What is a roadmap? "A plan that matches short-term and long-term goals with specific technology solutions to help meet those goals."

There is a fine line between moving too slow versus moving too fast. Modernizing your EUC services is a highly disruptive process, and organizations need to manage their resources and capabilities accordingly. You do not want to try and implement too many solutions at once, and not do a good job at any of them.

You will need to develop a roadmap that will help layout what the next few years will look like for your EUC strategy. This should take in account what your internal capacity is versus the need to bring in outside resources. This will likely be a discussion between how fast you need to move versus costs.

When developing your roadmap, it cannot be emphasized enough the importance of applications to your EUC project. Many of good EUC projects have been delayed or failed due to applications not being prioritized correctly. As you will learn in later parts of the book, applications are a pivotal part of your EUC services. Nearly every one of your use cases will require applications, whether they just need a single application or a suite of them presented. If applications are not prioritized properly it can cost you delays or force the project to make undesirable concessions.

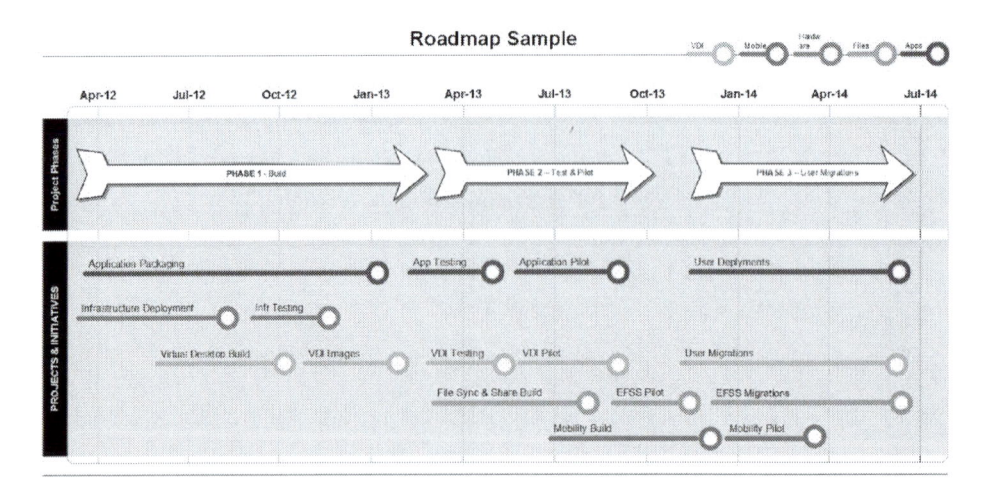

There are a number of different methods that can be used to visualize your roadmap. The example above is a simple way to see how the services would be deployed over a period of time. The sample was built from a template that is readily available online from different sites.

[2]
Use Cases

Your use cases will be very important to your EUC strategy and design process. If you do not understand and identify your use cases, you will just end up building EUC products with no idea if or how users will use them. That sounds like a really bad idea and sets the project up for failure. The process to identify your use cases can roughly be defined as "a methodology used in analysis to identify, clarify, and organize requirements."

Use cases are groups of users that require an EUC service(s) as it pertains to this book. Each use case will be comprised of a set of requirements. In your strategy or design phase, you will need to discover, identify, and qualify each of the use cases to validate if they will be a proper fit within your EUC offering.

It would be recommended to identify as many use cases as you can within your organization. Just because they are identified, though, does not mean that you have to consider them in scope for the project. As part of this process the project team should closely look at each use case and their requirements to understand if they are or are not a fit for this project. Another possibility is that they may not be a good fit today, but could be a better fit in the future when a service matures or some other factor.

How to identify use cases

The process to identify use cases is going to take place on several fronts. In all likelihood the business has already approached the IT organization with requests. These requests may come in many different methods, for example: The request may be clear and state that they have a group of offshore developers that they want to provide desktops to in a secure manner.

Requests can also come in the form of something more like this: The organization has several call center locations; each of these locations has hundreds of users; the organization has limited/no local support staff at these locations, and support operations can be challenging; these locations have multiple shifts of workers that share devices, this can sometimes complicate maintenance and other operations; the call centers fluctuate their staffing levels at different points during the calendar year, and it would be ideal to be able to deal with these changes in a better way; lastly, an easier method of deploying new users and to dramatically shorten the time to deploy a user would also be an objective.

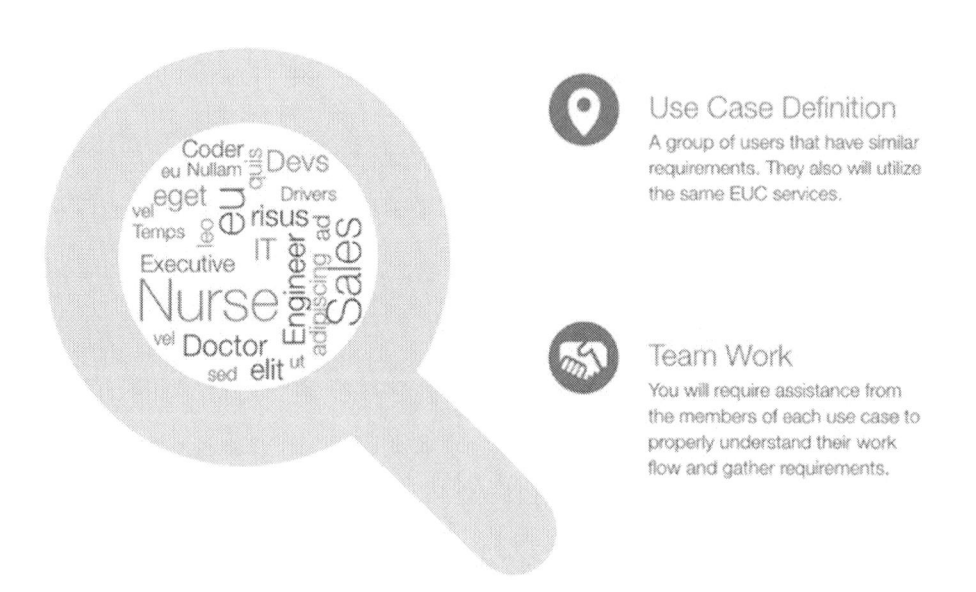

Use Case Definition
A group of users that have similar requirements. They also will utilize the same EUC services.

Team Work
You will require assistance from the members of each use case to properly understand their work flow and gather requirements.

Use Case Discovery

Not many use cases will come with that detailed of a description. You will need to spend time interviewing the requestors to gain further details. By having this discussion, you can discover what a typical developer's workflow with his/her desktop would be. Also, identify key applications the end users will need. This leads us into the next topic, what details you will need to know about each use case.

By working with someone in a leadership position within each use case, you are better able to understand what their daily workflow is. A workflow is how their jobs interface with the technology throughout the day. Once you have compiled your thoughts and assumptions, send an overview to the respective parties for validation. A few examples of these types of questions are listed below to get the process started.

- What type of device or endpoint do you use today?
- Do you have any known OS restrictions?
- What is a list of the applications used regularly?
- Where do you typically work from? (Office, remote, etc.)
- Can you explain any current limitations today?
- Do you have any feature requests?
- Do you use any connected devices or peripherals?

A good example of this would be a nurse. A typical nurse in a hospital goes from room to room visiting and working with different patients. Most of these rooms have a computer in them today or there is a computer on wheels (COW) that is pushed around with them.

The nurses are logging into and closing some type of medical records application, which is where they do the majority of their work. This primary application is used to look up patient history, take notes, and record all of their other interactions. They will typically need to print different documents, such as prescriptions or instructions, and these need to print to a nearby printer to save time and not get lost. This is just a brief summary, but you can quickly guess that if you did not have this type of input from each use case you would be blindly guessing.

14 | *Architecting EUC Solutions*

Those people in accounting probably just use spreadsheets all day and print stuff, right? Well maybe they send some emails also, that should be a really easy one to accomplish. What you might not know is that there is a group within accounting that uses high-end workstations and use a GPU to perform complex calculations.

Everyone in IT thinks that they know how all the different people in their organizations work and use the technology. This is because over time they have seen them, and worked on trouble tickets, and listened to complaints. Remember, though, that this does not make a server or even desktop admin an expert in how the business operates.

Use case attributes

Just identifying the use cases is not enough detail for a project of this type, or others. You will need to uncover the requirements and behaviors of each of the use cases to fully understand what services the use cases will require, and how you would architect a solution for them.

The list of requirements that you need or would want to identify can be pretty extensive. You need to cover topics such as: access, security, locations, applications, restrictions, peripherals, etc. The focus should be on things that the user needs to perform their job, items the business is concerned about for protecting their data, and should avoid the one offs from individual users. Remember that you are grouping things into larger use cases, and not catering to single users.

The following is a short list of requirements that may or may not apply to your project. This is a list of common attributes that have consistently come up over time. Use these suggestions to get your brain working to uncover others that will be critical to your use cases.

- EUC Service(s) - Which services will this use case consume?
- Endpoint - What type of device typically will this use case be using?
- Security - Do they require any restrictions? No USB access, disable copy/paste?
- Authentication – Is there a need for 2-Factor authentication or SAML support?
- Access Method - Will they be a LAN, WAN, VPN or Internet based user?
- Count - How many users are in this use case?
- Concurrency – How many users will be connected simultaneously? This will drive licensing decisions based on named user or concurrency models.
- Location - Will they be in a centralized location, remote office, road warrior, home user or across the world?
- Multi-media - Will the use case be a heavy user of rich video content?
- Application delivery method - Does the use case need ability to self-install applications?

The previous list is just a sampling of the type of data that you will want to collect about each of your use cases. There will be many more data points that will be important to your environment or use cases. The challenge is to identify what you care about and incorporate them into your use case analysis process.

The following is a table to illustrate a few of the example use cases with answers to some sample questions. A table-based view is a nice way to visualize the data for easier consumption.

ATTRIBUTES	CALL CENTER	FIELD SALES	ACCOUNTING	HR	VENDORS
Services	Desktop & Apps	Apps	Desktop & Apps	Desktop & Apps	Desktop & Apps
Endpoint	Thin Client	Laptop	PC	Thin Client	BYOD
Security	None	2-Factor Auth.	1. Disable USB access 2. Disable Copy/Past	1. Disable USB access 2. Disable Copy/Past	1. Disable USB access 2. Disable Copy/Past 3. Restrict network access to approved services
Access Method	LAN/WAN	VPN/Internet	LAN	LAN	Internet
Count	1000	150	25	20	100
Concurrency	50%	100%	100%	100%	20%
Location	5 sites	Remote	Corp Office	Corp Office	Remote
Multimedia	Minimal	Heavy	Minimal	Minimal	None
User installed apps	No	Yes	No	No	No

Finding Common Ground

When discovering use cases the list can rapidly grow; you can easily find yourself with a list of 30 plus items. This is not to say they are not valid use cases, but there is a fine line between real use cases and a detailed set of one-off use cases. I recommend that you initially record all of the use cases discovered, and collect their requirements. Next, examine the list to find commonality between some of the use cases. You will probably find that there are many common requirements between different use cases. They may have different names, but they need similar services and have the same requirements. This allows you to group them, and deal with the variances through one of the service layers.

It is often temping for organizations to go towards use cases with the largest group of users. Do not ignore use cases that can offer the largest impact by modernizing their EUC experience, even if the user base is smaller.

The image below illustrates this point. It started out with close to 20 use cases, through finding commonality in them they were reduced to just three use cases. Your data will ultimately drive this process. Ideally your use cases are very similar, or maybe they are not and you will not see that much of a reduction. Either way, it is important to prioritize them and not start too large of a project right at the beginning.

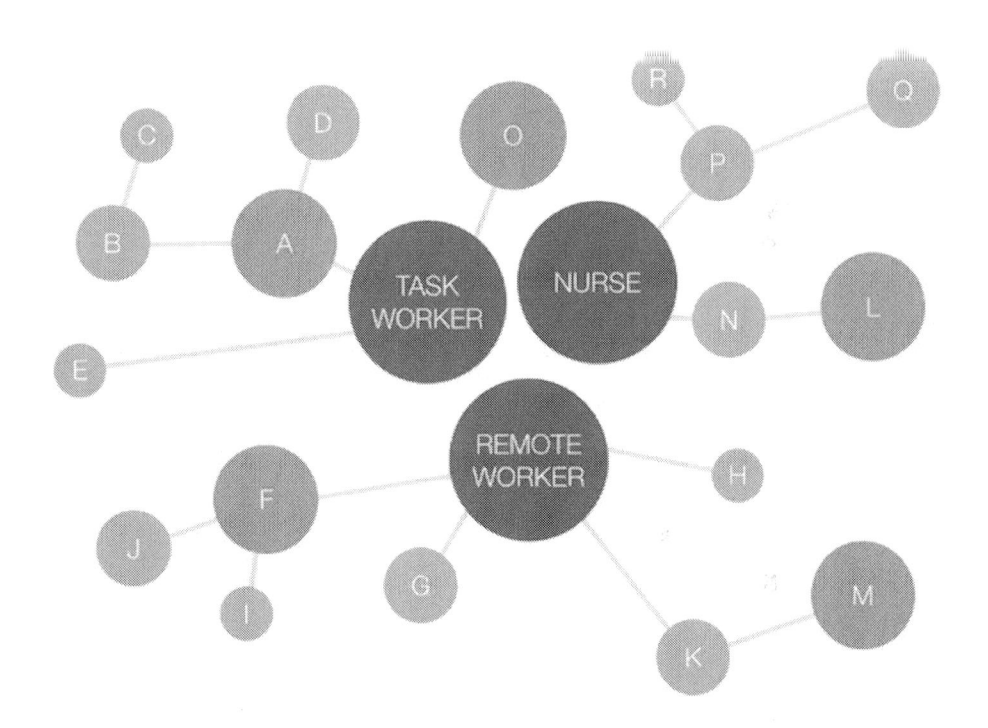

Find Use Case Commonality

An example of identifying use cases with similar requirements was created in the table below for demonstration. The accounting and human resources use cases have very much the same requirements. They both would need a virtual desktop of some form and would consume applications. The rest of the requirements also close. The main variance between the two will be the applications that each use case would use.

18 | *Architecting EUC Solutions*

ATTRIBUTES	CALL CENTER	FIELD SALES	ACCOUNTING	HR	VENDORS
Services	Desktop & Apps	Apps	Desktop & Apps	Desktop & Apps	Desktop & Apps
Endpoint	Thin Client	Laptop	PC	Thin Client	BYOD
Security	None	2-Factor Auth.	1. Disable USB access 2. Disable Copy/Past	1. Disable USB access 2. Disable Copy/Past	1. Disable USB access 2. Disable Copy/Past 3. Restrict network access to approved services
Access Method	LAN/WAN	VPN/Internet	LAN	LAN	Internet
Count	1000	150	25	20	100
Concurrency	50%	100%	100%	100%	20%
Location	5 sites	Remote	Corp Office	Corp Office	Remote
Multimedia	Minimal	Heavy	Minimal	Minimal	None
User installed apps	No	Yes	No	No	No

They will each likely use a group of common applications, but then require a set of departmental applications for their specific work. You will learn in the following chapters of the book how to design a flexible layered approach that will enable this level of granularity. The two use cases do have different endpoints, but nothing shown in the requirements gathering disqualifies either from working. Thus they remain compatible with each other. In all likelihood, they can use the same desktop image and just require the departmental applications to be presented to their users to meet the use cases requirements.

In previous project experiences, the lists of use cases have quickly grown to 20-30 items. After collection all of the requirements data and examining the list, the large number of use cases can almost always be collapsed to 5-10. This is done typically through building flexibility at the application layer; this will be covered further in Chapter 9 covering application management.

Summary

I cannot re-enforce enough how important identifying and understanding the use cases will be to the project and your design process. If you do not understand the requirements of users, you will be unable to properly design for them. You must understand the why before moving on to the how and when.

[3]
Starting the Design Process

At this point, this book has covered the introduction to EUC to explain the foundation of services that will be offered as part of the strategy and design being developed. As part of the strategy development you have selected which services you intend to offer to your users. The roadmap that you should have also developed as part of the process will help you prioritize the order of the services and other parts of the EUC solution.

The use case definition process that you have or will go through is going to identify who and how they will be consuming the EUC services. As part of the use case process, the requirements of each use case were captured in detail. These requirements are going to heavily guide your EUC vendor selection, and be heavily factored into your upcoming design decisions that will be made throughout the design process.

Before diving fully into the design phase it's important to have the following items completed. If these are left uncompleted you run the risk of false starting or having to circle back too many times:

- Strategy (Which EUC services)
- Roadmap
- Objectives, Constraints, Risks, and Assumptions details
- Use cases definition
- EUC vendor selection

With these prerequisites completed you are ready to start working on your detailed design.

Project Requirements

In the strategy phase the project team already defined the requirements. These will need to be revisited at the start of the design phase of your project. You will need to make sure that the constraints, risks, objectives, and assumptions still hold true entering the design phase.

You may find that some of these requirements have changed or gone away. An example of this might be that an assumption that was made in the strategy phase of the project is now a known fact or the item has been completed prior to the design starting. You could also find that a previous constraint has been removed. For example, you are no longer required to only consider storage options from the incumbent vendor.

In the strategy phase, you were looking at the higher levels of what types of services would be provided, and what problems might the strategy solve. As part of the design phase, you will likely discover additional requirements. In the design phase you will be focused on more detailed technical discussions and those carry with them a new set of requirements.

The design phase should start with a final review of the approved strategy, and ensure that all members of the project team are in agreement. You should talk through the requirements identified in the strategy phase and discuss if any should be removed or change. Once the existing requirements have been discussed the focus should shift to identifying the new design focused requirements.

To provide examples, the samples from the Strategy section will be changed to reflect new Objectives, Constraints, Risks, and Assumptions that were discovered in the design phase. These are again a small sampling to show what the design level examples might look like.

Objectives
- Improve security
- Allow for company owned devices and BYOD
- Provide the same user experience from any location
- Present applications to any device

Constraints
- Must use existing internet connectivity
- Cannot migrate users during peak seasons
- Must use existing 2-Factor authentication method for external connections
- Only Citrix products can be used in the solution

Risks
- Cannot hire external resources for deployment work
- Lack of flash storage
- Current staff has no Citrix experience

Assumptions
- Deployment team will be trained on Citrix prior to deployment
- Customer will hire resources to meet deadlines
- New EUC team will be created

With the projects requirements detailed at the design level, you are now ready to continue on with the design discussions and process.

Revisit Use Case Requirements

Similar to revising the requirements at the start of the design phase, you will want to also take another pass at the use case list and definitions. Typically, the first pass use case definition is done during the strategy phase, and the level of detail required at the level is not the same that is needed to complete a detailed design.

Depending on how detailed your use case requirement definition process was, it would be recommended that it be at least reviewed with business leaders during the design phase of the project. There may have also been new use cases that were identified. These new use cases will have to be either included within the design or excluded with details explaining why.

Each use case is going to need a lots of detail about how it will be used, what the security requirements are, and what products they will use to provide the services being consumed. These are going to drive design discussions that lead to design decisions of how you will architect the products to deliver on the requirements.

This level of detail will be discussed throughout the book in the different design chapters for each type of service and related topics. This added detail will help define details such as whether a use case will require a dedicate pool of desktops or can it share a pool with other use cases with similar requirements; what types of policies within the products and group policy will be required to control the behavior, security, and performance of the use cases.

Does a use case like a medical transcription require a special foot pedal? These are the questions that will be asked about each use case. This type of requirement can drive what type of endpoint the use case would be able to use, and whether the transcription application can be directly presented to an endpoint or will the use case require a full virtual desktop experience.

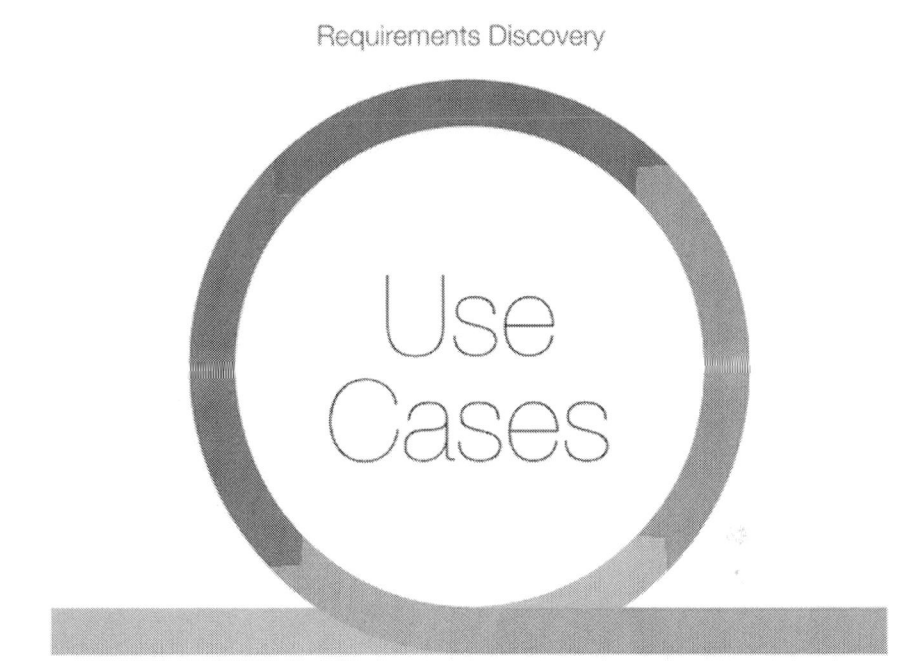

Revisit Use Case Requirements

Hopefully it is clear that the use case requirements will drive your design decision just as much as the objectives and requirements of the project. So understanding these is critical, because an EUC design is far more complicated than deciding that you are just going to use RDSH to present 40 applications and will provide Windows 7 and Windows 8 virtual desktops to anyone that requests them.

Design Layers

Within any design project or in Enterprise Architecture, there are three layers of a design. These three layers are there to provide different levels of detail that is intend to communicate the designs purpose to different members of the business, project team and leadership. The layers include:

- Conceptual Design - This layer provides an explanation of the design in terms that are not deeply technical. Conceptual design is painting the picture of what the design is going to do, without the need to explain the how.
- Logical Design - This layer begins to dig in a bit deeper, but still not identify specific product names. This level of detail is going to explain how the services would be provided. Such as a virtual desktop with virtualized applications will meet these requirements.
- Physical Design - This layer provides detailed descriptions of the design with specific details about products and their interactions and dependencies.

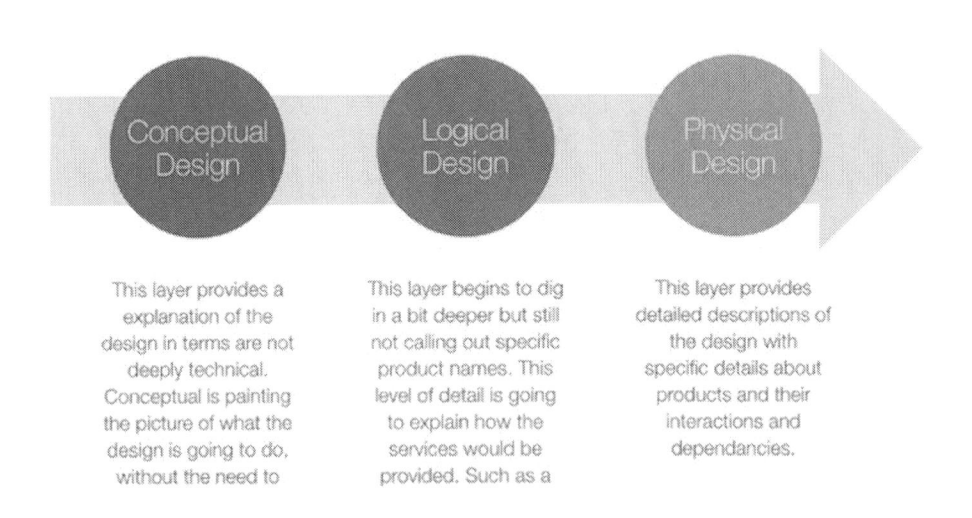

Conceptual Design	Logical Design	Physical Design
This layer provides a explanation of the design in terms are not deeply technical. Conceptual is painting the picture of what the design is going to do, without the need to	This layer begins to dig in a bit deeper but still not calling out specific product names. This level of detail is going to explain how the services would be provided. Such as a	This layer provides detailed descriptions of the design with specific details about products and their interactions and dependancies.

Now that you have some understanding of the different layers that are possible within a design, you might be wondering if all these layers are really necessary. To properly design your EUC offerings and communicate with the business, you will need all of these design layers to be successful. The following sections will explain why each of these design layers will be valuable to different parties.

Conceptual Layer

The conceptual design is an important part of a design project. This is essentially your marketing material for your design project. At this level you are taking the business objective and requirements and turning them into a design story that the business can consume. This means non-technical people should be able to understand the goals and outcomes of your EUC project. You are using this to explain what the solution should do, and not killing them with technical jargon. The conceptual design is sort of an executive summary of the project in some ways. It will be used to offer an explanation of what the business should expect from the solution. Some organizations may use it to campaign for funding to move into the detailed design and deployment phases.

Since you are just talking about business level details, you will have a good amount of freedom in what is actually designed for. You will not be talking about specific products and vendors in the conceptual design, so as long as your final design meets the business needs. There should not be any complaints about you using Vendor A versus Vendor B in the final solution. Since you got approval of the conceptual design in the beginning, all you need to do is deliver on what is included in the strategically defined outcomes, and you will have the freedom to design within these details.

The conceptual design may be its own document or simply could be included in the early part of your all-encompassing design documentation. Through the years, I have seen both ways used by organizations. I, however, usually prefer a separate conceptual document. This is completed before the other design layers are done, and does not provide details about the other design layers that might confuse non-technical people and cause un-needed questions. Think of this document as your marketing brochure, and it will be used in your campaign to explain the solution to the business and management without dropping a 100 plus page document on their desk.

Logical Layer

In the logical design layer, you start to dig a bit deeper into the design elements. You are not focusing on specific products at this design layer. The goal is to be designing the solution to meet the requirements, and not be too focused on trying to work around the limitations certain products might present. It is common that by this time most organizations have already made their product decision, though this is not required.

As you begin to connect the dots between the requirements identified in earlier stages to how they will be satisfied in your design, you will be asking a lot of questions. For example, you have a requirement of 5 Nines of availability that translates to roughly 5 minutes of unplanned down time per year. That is very little breathing room to meet your service level agreement (SLA), so you had better think of all the different pieces of the solution to ensure they have the highest levels of redundancy.

You are going to be asking yourself and the team if the organization can meet 5 nines with a single data center. Are we risking failure by only adding enough resources to survive one possible failure or are we require protecting against multiple simultaneous failures? Does there need to be two or three data centers to host the solution actively in to meet these guarantees? Within each of the data centers, are there going to be database requirements for different products? What levels of protection and redundancy will you need to design for? Will you require database clusters? If so what type of database and clustering technology will meet your requirements?

If you are working with other architects as a team designing this solution, regular meetings are recommended with healthy doses of white boarding sessions. This type of collaboration keeps the team focused and is great at working through alternatives to these design choices. If you are working alone, it would still be a good idea to do some white boarding as visualizing things may help, along with putting your thoughts down on paper so you do not miss any. For projects of this size, they encompass a wide set of skills required and the recommendation would be to utilize an architecture team that brings various skill sets to the table. It is an incredibly difficult challenge to expect a single architect to provide all of the required design skills for a project that includes many of these EUC services.

Physical Layer

At this physical design layer, you are now connecting all of the previous discussions and choices with the products that will ultimately be implemented. You may now know that Horizon View will be providing your virtual desktops, and based upon choices made in the logical layer you will now document the specific Horizon design choices. Are there any limitations within the product decision that affects the potential multi-data center design choice for high availability? In the case of Horizon, yes. Knowing the current product, one will need to design for a Horizon View pod deployment within each data center site. This will require you to decide if you will isolate these discrete environments from your end users, and make them look and feel as one large pool of resources.

You know that you have F5 load balancers available to you, and there are options for presenting a single URL to users and use rules to direct them to the desired data center. This level of detail would have not been discussed in the previous design layers, but must be documented here so that the implementers of the design have the level of details to deploy the architecture team's vision.

In the logical layer, it was briefly brought up about the database alternative discussion. Now that you know what product you are dealing with, you can document the specific instructions. You know that Horizon only supports Microsoft SQL for databases. You will have the option of Failover cluster or AlwaysOn cluster for providing database high availability. You will need to research which options Horizon supports or works with. In some circumstances you may choose to select an alternative that is not explicitly called out as supported by the vendor. It may still work if the organization is willing to accept this risk.

As the design decisions are made, it is the goal to try and map them back to the requirements, constraints, and assumptions documented earlier. This will help illustrate why decisions were made for one alternative over another, and help paint the picture for others reading or reviewing the design.

Depending on who is writing the design and documents, choices can easily be lost in the thousands of words. To make decisions clear they should be specifically pointed out for those reading or reviewing the design document.

> *Design decision – The call center use case with 2000 users will use non-persistent desktops with application layering.*

Most choices might not be this simple, but the above design decision was made to satisfy both the requirement to create a solution that reduced effort for operating system and application updates. Also, this design decision can be linked back to another requirement of reducing security risks, by not allowing users to save data and refreshing desktops at logoff.

The best way to link the decision to the project requirements is to explain things in detail. Others have simply listed that the decision matches to requirement 1 or R1. While this links the two things together, it may not go into enough detail to understand why and how they are tied together.

The diagram below is a visual simply of mapping decisions back to project requirements. In a design document, it probably will not be a diagram like this, rather more of a call-out within the document. You have the option to handle this in any manner that fits the style or formats used within the organization.

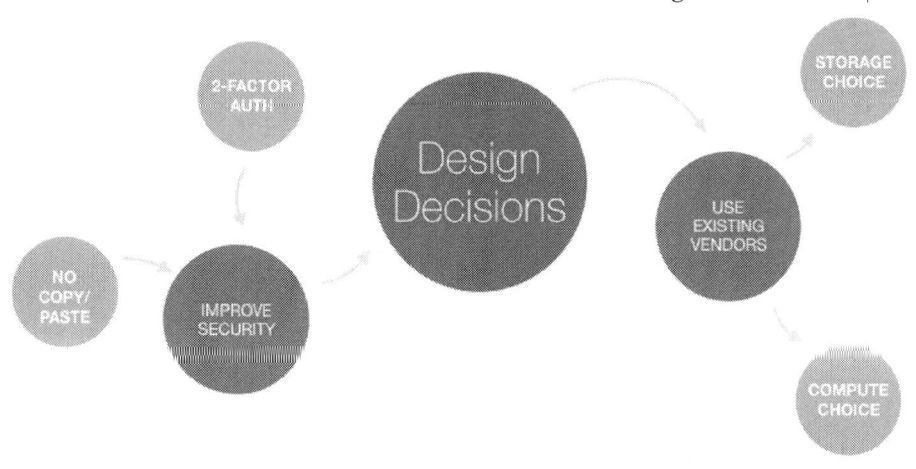

Summary

This chapter was to provide you with some guidance on how to start and proceed through the design thought process. The goal was to start to point your mind in the right direction and will help you follow the specific topics in the remaining chapters of this book.

[4]
Pilots and Proof of Concepts

It can be a common request from business leaders, application owners, and IT team members to question if the technology really works as advertised. Another common question is will it work in our environment. These often lead to Proof of Concepts (POC) and Pilots. A short definition of each of these activities is listed below before each is covered in more depth afterwards.

- **Proof of Concept** - a demonstration to verify that certain concepts or theories have the potential for real-world application. POC is therefore a prototype that is designed to determine feasibility, but does not represent deliverables.
- **Pilot** - refers to an initial roll-out of a system into production, targeting a limited scope of the intended final solution. The scope may be limited by the number of users who can access the system, the business processes affected, the business partners involved, or other restrictions as appropriate to the domain. The purpose of a pilot project is to test, often in a production environment.

Proof of Concepts

It's 2016, even people on the moon should understand the value of most of the mobility products today. If not by product name, then people should be able to talk to them about the services, these are terms and features they should understand.

Throughout this book it will continue to reference the EUC services that are being covered. This is a great way to discuss EUC with both the business side and the IT side of your organization. By discussing services and requirements you will spend less time debating one product versus another. The real conversation should be on what the business would like to deliver to the end users.

These days there is very little to be gained by running your own POC. History has seen too many customers try to throw together a POC of a proposed EUC solution; the failure rate is extremely high. There are a number of reasons that customer driven POCs fail, and many vendor driven POCs are not much more successful. The following is a list of top reasons that POCs will fail or not deliver the desired results.

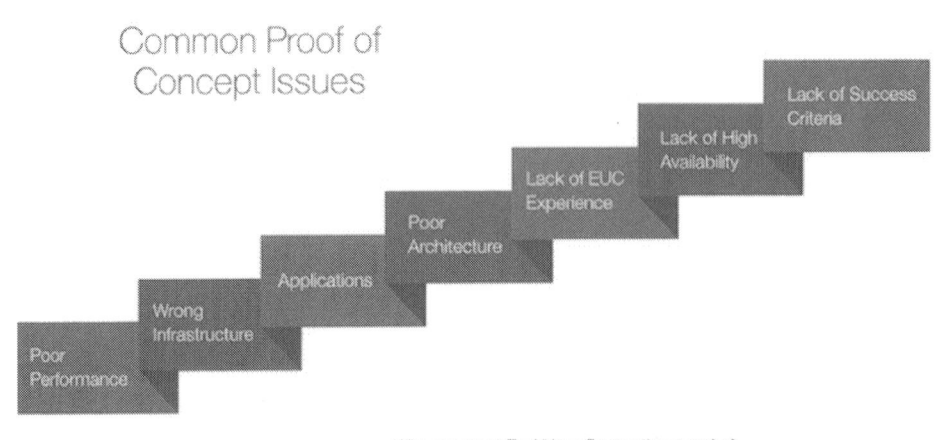

Common Proof of Concept Issues

- Poor Performance
- Wrong Infrastructure
- Applications
- Poor Architecture
- Lack of EUC Experience
- Lack of High Availability
- Lack of Success Criteria

Why are most End User Computing proof of concept trials failing to succeed?

Poor Performance - This is one of the top sins in the POC world. If you are successful in building the EUC services in which you want to POC, but they perform badly, all the work you did was for nothing. In all likelihood you have probably done more harm than good because your users and leadership are now poisoned with a poor user experience. This will directly affect their perception of what the products and services have to offer.

Wrong Infrastructure - It might seem obvious, but this closely ties into the previous point about poor performance. If you intend on using existing infrastructure or legacy gear that was retired already you are destined to fail. Unless you just purchased the testing gear and it closely resembles the requirements of your final design, you will not be able to offer the expected performance and behavior of the desired state design environment. You are better off not doing a POC than doing it wrong.

By using improper infrastructure not only will it affect performance, but will also not reflect the consolidation that you expect, along with a different management and operational experience. These are all important in showcasing the value of your design.

Applications - Right up there with using the wrong infrastructure is being unprepared for the application parts of a POC. If you intend to have any applications as part of the POC, then this is critical. Typical POCs attempt to attach the infrastructure and VDI together, and applications are an afterthought that blindsides participants at the end of the project.

Applications are critical to your overall EUC strategy and design as highlighted in Chapter 1. Applications will be further covered in Chapter 9. There may be some use cases that only require application presentation; you may need to test application presentation, application layering, and other strategies. These will be critical to test for management, consumption, and performance. The application part of a POC can easily consume the most time to prepare and get right. So this cannot be overlooked or rushed.

Poor Architecture - Much like using the wrong infrastructure, if you cut corners when architecting the management and presentation layers within the POC it will show up in your results. Combining layers into a single server for a POC may sound like it is easier and the right thing, but it may have negative results. For example, to make external access testing easier, people have skipped using proper access path designs and simply exposed an internal server in order to allow these connections. While this is faster, it potentially changes the user experience. You could lose the opportunity to learn from the POC process and end up getting surprised by items you missed when designing and deploying the final solution.

Lack of EUC Experience - EUC is not like server virtualization, so asking that team to run an EUC POC is not recommended. The server team is typically not prepared to understand and support desktop services and applications. These items, along with brokering and presentation layers, is going to be reflected in the results. You should look to acquire these skills internal or externally before taking on such an effort.

Lack of High Availability - This item builds on the previous poor architecture topic. If you build a POC environment that does not offer high availability and has several single point of failures (SPOF), it will come back to haunt you. You are asking users to test and contribute to the success of this project, and if parts of the environment are unavailable because of a single failure or due to maintenance, you are going to hear about it. They are also going to talk to others and assume that if deployed, the product implementation would likely suffer from these interruptions as well. This is not how you want to build momentum and affect the marketing of your project.

Lack of Success Criteria – EUC history has seen a large number of POCs go bad because a lack of success factors. This happens when organizations and vendors are not clear and definitive about what they are testing. Also, the practice of using unrealistic POC testing methods: IOMeter for EUC does not make a realistic test so align your POC with the outcome you're looking for.

Externally Driven POC

If doing a POC is required at your organization, an option to do this would be to look for another method of accomplishing the goal. Today pretty much all of the EUC software vendors mentioned earlier have demo environments that can be utilized for customers wishing to test or prove something out. Many of these can be assigned for a period of time to allow customer to test drive the solution.

If the vendor does not have the ability to provide these POC environments, the next option would be to inquire with your other technology partners. Many partners have lab environments that customers can use for these types of POC requests and may even provide more flexibility than the vendor environments can offer. Either way these two options are more likely to produce the outcome that you are looking to demonstrate. They will also be considerably less resource intensive on your organization's teams.

In the end, most understand that you may have to provide a POC of some sort to sell the business on the technology to get a project funded. Just consider all of your options before jumping into the POC blindly.

Pilots

Often projects have used a pilot as nothing more than a POC in disguise. This does a disservice to your team and the project. By the time you reach the pilot stage you should fully understand your EUC strategy, and should also have a fully baked EUC design completed. Hopefully, your project is at least partially funded so that you can have the best chance of succeeding.

If you refer to the pilot definition above, "an initial roll-out of a system into production", then you notice the reference to production in the definition. The IT world should rebrand pilots as "Production Pilot". This would better reflect the intended goals and set proper expectations.

To increase your chances of having a successful pilot, you should be building a pilot sized implementation of your desired state EUC design. This means that much like it was talked about earlier in the POC section, that using old or shared infrastructure can lead to poor results. The pilot phase is intended to be production, and should perform like production, as well as follow the operational processes that you will use in production.

This means a pilot infrastructure build must be a scaled down version of the future desired state. Sizing a pilot is important. The scope of a pilot should be tightly controlled to prevent scope creep, and it should also manage user experience. During the pilot phase you are looking to find any last minute surprises that were not previously uncovered, and also build momentum for the EUC services as you approach a larger deployment. The importance of having a good reputation will be critical in getting each use case to buy into your EUC solution, and not resist being migrated to these new services.

The goal of your pilot is to pick a single use case or a small subset of the use cases. This will allow you to manage expectations and also increase the chances for success. By selecting a subset of use cases you are controlling what EUC services and support services need to be implemented for the pilot. For example, if you try and pilot 10 of the use cases that require virtual desktops, you will likely find yourself in a bind when it comes to the applications that these use cases require. Can you properly package and have the diverse set of applications that each of the use cases require for the pilot phase? Usually not, this is a real sticking point for many customers.

Also, out of the pilot use cases that are selected, you should not open it up to the full user count of each group. You should be targeting a small number of users in each use case. Your goal here is to not deploy these use cases in full, but rather to slowly ramp them up in a production environment that allows you to control the scope and perception. While learning about any details that you might have not expected in the previous phases.

Picking the right Pilot Use Cases

Picking the wrong use cases for your pilot users can negatively affect the process and project. Do not make a wrong choice and get bulldozed over.

This approach lends itself to selecting your easier use cases and also use cases that do not have your most difficult to please and vocal customers in. Let's face it, for those of you in IT that have worked with doctors, lawyers, and executives, they can sometimes not be the easiest set of people to please. If you mess-up with these use cases, you are going to suffer from a poor perception that you will have to eventually overcome.

Summary

While many do not see a lot of value in POCs anymore, a production pilot will be very important to your success. How you approach your production pilot will greatly affect what the results are. If you manage a selective number of use cases and user counts within them, this will help control the quality of your pilot. Also it must be on production quality infrastructure that at minimum reflects a scaled down version of the desired state design.

Your production pilot is a bit like your running someone's presidential campaign. The team is responsible to delivering the right EUC message and experience and you need to carefully manage the marketing to not have negative poll results. After all you want your EUC project to get elected and fully funded.

[5]
Desktop Assessments

Understanding your environment is a critical part of any EUC project. A desktop assessment will help provide the details that organizations need in order to properly design for their requirements. The assessment phase is not an easy stage, and often there is an expense to performing an assessment.

For this reason, history has seen many organizations try and move forward without doing a proper assessment. By skipping the assessment phase, organizations are opening themselves up to several risks. Without proper details, their EUC project will be susceptible to sizing errors, performance troubles, and time delays. Any one of those can seriously derail any project, and will cause your end users to turn against the project. Another thing you want to avoid is creating a bad user experience; this will affect all parts of the deployment.

What are the Options?

To gather this data it will take either a lot of effort or a specialized tool. There are essentially three methods for this approach. The options would be:
- A manual labor effort
- A survey based effort
- A purpose created tool

The manual effort would rely on a team of technical people that are doing manual discovery, using scripts to pull data, or using a number of different tools to grab different blocks of data. This is both a time consuming and potentially an error prone task to undertake.

A survey-based approach is one that has probably not been seen in the wild very often. The idea is a questionnaire is prepared and distributed to leaders within each of your use cases. They would attempt to answer your questions and explain how each user group uses the technology. The problem here, is without any guidance, you may get incorrect answers or partially filled out surveys. The other danger is some percentage will not fill them out at all. The idea of this approach is correct that the project team needs their input, but this is the wrong approach.

Assessment Tools

The information that needs to be gathered is not something that can be easily pieced together from multiple tools. Many of these details are not available in most types of monitoring tools, and a scattered approach is not going to provide the results that you will find useful.

To accomplish a proper assessment, you will need to use a tool that was designed for this purpose. There are now several good ones available on the market today. They do a good job of gathering details and they provide a large set of predefined reports to make getting the data out of the tool easy.

Four of the leading desktop assessment tools are:

- **Liquidware Labs Stratusphere Fit** - Uses an OS based agent to gather details on resource usable and applications. The same agent can be used for fitting the post deployment monitoring product.

- **Lakeside SysTrack** - Gathers data on monitored endpoints similar to other tools to aid in the design and planning of a VDI deployment.
- **uberAgent** - A plugin that uses Splunk to collect data. The combination has proven powerful. It can be very helpful in the upfront sizing phase, and also in the ongoing monitoring of your environment.
- **Microsoft Assessment and Planning Toolkit (MAP)** – Existing tool that has been extended to collect desktop data to aid in sizing EUC environments.

Who will run the assessment tool for you? While some customers may be willing to invest the time into learning one of these tools, it will lengthen the time it takes to complete this assessment phase. They also require the expertise to understand some of the data and how your data points compare to other organizations in your vertical or to others in general.

Because of this, these desktop assessments are typically performed by a vendor or partner. They will have experience in running these for other organizations, and will be able to quickly interpret the data. This will help you understand how it will affect your design sizing. If you, as a customer, elect to go this process alone, there will likely be some type of licensing cost from the tool vendor.

How Long Does the Process Take?

You typically want to collect a month's worth of data to ensure that you do not miss any peak periods in the environment. More than 30 days can be collected, but there will likely be less benefit to collecting this additional amount of data unless there is another purpose for it. Collecting less than 30 days of data can lead to an incomplete assessment of the environment. It is very common for sales teams to want to push a customer to keep things moving along, and only collects one to two weeks worth of data. Some data is certainly better than no data, but it is a disservice to the project to try and rush this activity.

44 | *Architecting EUC Solutions*

As the architect or executive sponsor for this EUC project, you may need to fight for a proper collection period duration. During the collection window there should be at least one check point, if not multiple ones, to ensure that the data is being collected from the endpoints included in the assessment. Sometimes agents stop or there are communications troubles and data is not being collected or uploaded. You do not want to reach the end of your collection period and find out there is little there and you have to start again.

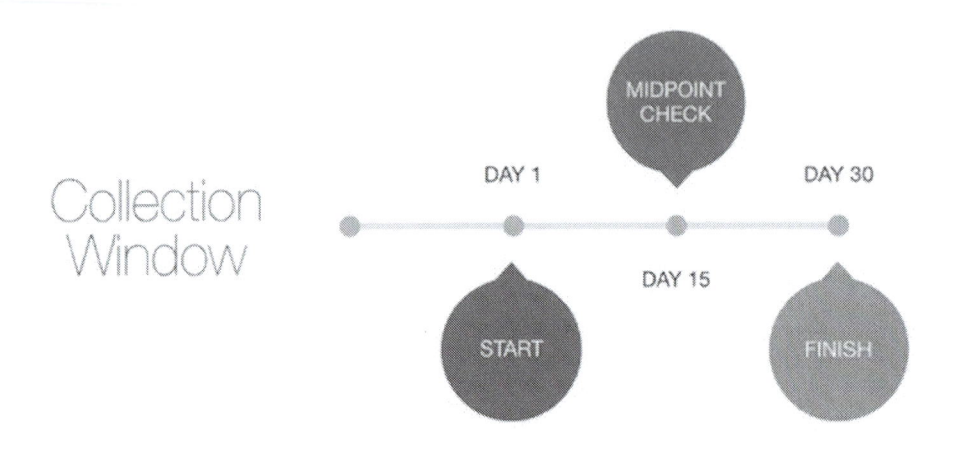

Collection Window

DAY 1 — MIDPOINT CHECK — DAY 30
START — DAY 15 — FINISH

Today's desktops and the ones purchased for the last several years are very powerful. They provide far more computing power than a majority of business users need. The average desktop has a CPU with two or more cores and likely has 2-4 GB of memory, if not more. Your users probably on average use only a fraction of this power. If you intend to mirror this configuration in your virtual desktops, then you will suffer the same over-provisioning errors that the server admins that took this approach in the early VMware days.

To get the right information, you are going to need the right tool, and also figure to out what types of information you should be gathering in the first place.

What Do You Want to Discover?

So hopefully by now it is clear why you should be performing a desktop assessment. But what type of data should you be discovering from your desktop environment? The primary goal is to gather real sizing data to be used in the design of the virtual environment. To accomplish this, the resource usage is going to be the main target.

The assessment should gather performance data for a window of usage, typically for the physical computers but also can include virtual machines. As mentioned earlier, the window cannot be too small as you want to account for a normal work cycle that would include peak points of work during the month.

You will likely be trying to collect data from a number of different use cases for your design. Before deploying the agents from the assessment tool, the project team will need to determine from which use cases they wish to collect desktop data. To achieve a good testing sample, you will want a number of endpoints within each use case. Ideally you might want between 20 to 100 endpoints per use case, depending on the size of your organization. If you can do more per use case, that is fine, generally less is not better. The goal here is to ensure that one is getting a good sample from multiple users within each use case. To accomplish this there is a bit of planning that goes into this, before just pushing out the agent onto a bunch of endpoints.

As you deploy the solution, you will be using the inventory and mapping of endpoints to use cases from which you collected the data. It will be important to try and group the physical computers that you are collecting data from into logical groups that translate back to your use cases. Most of these tools have the ability to create groupings of endpoints and tag the agent so that it belongs to one of these groups, which eventually translate back to a use case. This will allow reports to be pulled that will illustrate the resource requirements for each use case. You take these reports, along with the estimated user counts, for each use case to perform the math to arrive at the total resource requirements for each use case.

46 | *Architecting EUC Solutions*

The primary performance points that one should be looking to gather for sizing is focused on CPU usage, memory usage, disk usage and possibly GPU usage, which will show us the performance needs. These are the three main resource buckets that will affect how the virtual desktops are sized, which will affect how the host servers are sized and architected for failover and such.

When looking at disk IOPS there is going to be an average of all desktops within each use case. There will also be a peak average, as well as the highest IOPS consumer. As part of the discovery, you should understand what types of disks are in the physical devices for which that data is being collected. This will help set expectations and account for any numbers that may be skewed by having devices with SSD when not required.

You can get these details out of the selected discovery tool. This will allow the team to plan for what should be expected on an average day, during predictable peak times during the day or week, and also make use aware of any outliers that are consuming more resources than normal users. You should always understand peak requirements and size your storage to scale against those numbers.

This data will then be used when you later design the desktop pools and hosts that the desktops will run on. There will be density, high availability, and performance decisions made by you that will be affected by the data gathered in the assessment.

The following list is a sample of some of the main performance resource data points that you will be collecting for examination:

- CPU used Peak/Average
- Memory used Peak/Average
- Disk IOPS Peak/Average
- Disk Read/Write percentages
- Network bandwidth used

As part of the data collections, you should also develop a desktop baseline for the existing environment. This will help you in comparing the legacy environment with your newly deployed virtual environment. This will also enable you to tune your deployment to make sure it performs the same or better than the previous physical devices. It will provide you with concrete data when addressing user complaints about performance being worse than the old environment. It would also be a goal to establish a new baseline of performance once the new virtual environment is established, and settled in to understand when anomalies occur.

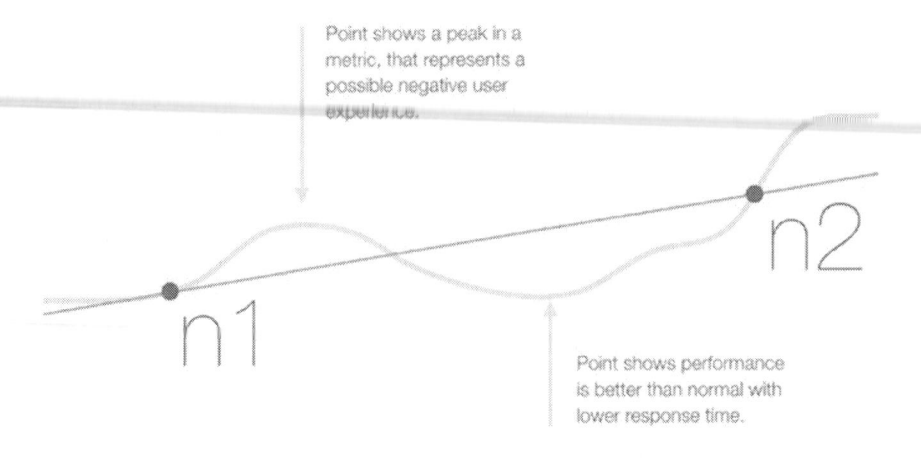

Point shows a peak in a metric, that represents a possible negative user experience.

n1

n2

Point shows performance is better than normal with lower response time.

The blue line represent our baseline or normal performance level. The gray line illustrates how our performance increases or decreases over time, helping understand how the environment is performing.

Application Discovery

Along with the resources that will be required for each of the use cases within your design, you are going to need to develop an understanding of the applications, Unless you are lucky enough to have use cases that are very narrow and have a finite set of applications, like a call center, you are going to need to gather as much detail about the applications as is relevant for the project.

A complete application inventory is going to be very important. You will need to know what applications are installed, and which ones are being used on a regular basis. There will likely be multiple versions of several applications installed and running within the environment. The design will need to account for this or look to reduce the number of versions if possible.

Not to be ignored is discovering the application owner for each one discovered, as well as an understanding of critical details around licensing, upgrades, and installation details. All of which will be covered in more detail in Chapter 9.

With any modern desktop PC or laptop there are going to be a set of less-than-desirable vendor applications that are installed in the image that are worthless or will be not needed in a virtualized environment. These could be vendor support tools, software to update firmware on a physical device, useless free applications and other software that the PC vendor probably received money to place in the build. You will need to identify these and account for them, so they do not negatively affect your design.

It will be important to factor in the use cases that were covered in Chapter 2 earlier. You will need to understand the applications that are used within each use case. This will affect the application management for each use case and potentially the resources required for each use case. It will be helpful if the tool that you choose for your assessment can group users that you will be monitoring by defined use cases. This way when you report on details they will be more useful.

Applications can be categorized in several different ways. A simple method would be to find out which applications every use case will use. Those could be considered your enterprise applications. Then applications that are only used within a single use case could be referred to as departmental applications. Lastly, applications that are only used by a subset of users can be referred to as individual applications.

There could be other ways to categorize applications within your environment; these are just to provide some food for thought. You can group them up however it makes sense for your design; the point is that you are going to need to do it.

50 | *Architecting EUC Solutions*

USE CASES	ENTERPRISE APPS	DEPARTMENT APPS	INDIVIDUAL APPS
Sales	Ms Office Adobe Acrobat	CRM Quoting app	Evernote
Call Center	Adobe Acrobat Reader	Call center app	None
IT Staff	MS Office Acrobat Reader	Service desk app Monitoring app	Notepad ++ Storage mgmt tools Cisco network tool

Summary

It cannot be said enough that having real data to make your design and sizing decisions off is important. You can try and size off of averages and industry defined use cases, but you are opening yourself up to risk by finding your use cases may not be anywhere close to them.

Many customers over time have focused too heavily on desktop sizing and ignored the application part of the assessment only to have it haunt them later, cause serious project delays or affect the operational benefits of the design.

If you don't properly discover, define and group applications you will end up with a mess. Seen too many customers just widely present applications to all users because of lack of information or effort. You will want to properly assign applications based on use case to control the access and operations of your applications, this will be discussed further in Chapter 9.

[6]
Virtual Desktops

When it comes to EUC, IT departments are tasked with two main tasks. The first is delivering the business applications and data to the users. The second is deploying and maintaining the devices that employees use to access those applications and data.

Traditionally, this has meant managing and deploying applications to physical devices, such as desktops and laptops. These devices were usually owned or leased, by the company. Tools existed to manage desktops and laptops, but they are often complicated and require significant investment in time and infrastructure to get deployed.

When that machine breaks, a user will not be productive until that machine is fixed. If it cannot be fixed, or if the machine has reached the end of its life, IT will need to replace the hardware and spend time recovering data and reinstalling the user's applications.

With increased demand for working remote and the advent of smartphones and tablets, users also want the ability to work anywhere from the device of their choice. It can be difficult for IT departments to deliver secure solutions to these requests so long as the end user is tightly coupled to the physical computer that they are assigned.

How Virtualization Helps

Virtualization offers a solution to this problem. When you virtualize the desktop OS and place it in the data center, it becomes easier to deliver secure managed desktops to users wherever they might be. The endpoint device no longer matters and users have the freedom to work from any device of their choice.

Virtualizing the desktop OS gives the desktop administrators options in how they architect and administer the environment. These options include how the virtual desktops are deployed, managed, and updated or patched. The end result can look like anything from just-in-time desktops that are disposed of when the user logs out to full virtual machines (VMs) that are managed the same as traditional physical desktops.

Virtual desktop deployments are often described one of two ways. They are either persistent or non-persistent. Non-persistent desktops can be further broken down into two categories – machines where the user state does not persist after login, and machines that are removed or reverted back to a known good state after the user is finished with it. There are also a number of different ways to deploy virtual desktops that will impact the decision to do persistent and non-persistent desktops.

Desktop Types

There are a primarily three different ways to deploy Windows desktops virtually. While most of these methods can be used for persistent or non-persistent desktops or user experience, some methods are better suited for one type.

The three primary methods to deploying virtual desktops that will be discussed in detail through the rest of this chapter and are:

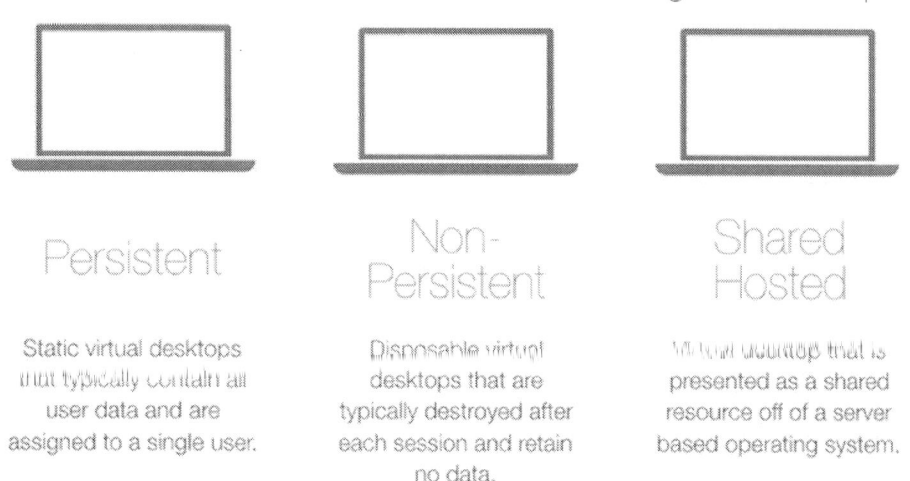

Persistent	Non-Persistent	Shared Hosted
Static virtual desktops that typically contain all user data and are assigned to a single user.	Disposable virtual desktops that are typically destroyed after each session and retain no data.	Virtual desktops that is presented as a shared resource off of a server based operating system.

Persistent Desktops

The term persistent desktop implies that everything about the users profile, data and applications persists between sessions and is typically tied to a single virtual desktop. This is very much like the desktop and laptop computers that are deployed to office workers. That machine is typically assigned to a single user, and when that user restarts or logs off, their settings and applications are retained. The next time they turn it on and log in, their user profile is loaded and all of their settings and applications are available to use. If system updates or new applications need to be deployed, there are a number of systems that can manage this for administrators so they do not need to visit each workstation to perform software installations.

Persistent virtual desktops look and behave just like their physical counterparts. Another name for persistent virtual desktop infrastructure (VDI) is full clone desktops. Each desktop is an exact and full clone of the template or VM that it was copied from. Each virtual desktop is dedicated to an end user, and when the user is done with the VM, their settings and applications are retained. The tools that are used for managing physical endpoints can also manage persistent virtual desktops, such as Microsoft Systems Center Configuration Manager (SCCM/Config Manager), VMware Mirage, or other PC Lifecycle.

It is important to understand that in persistent full clone desktops, both the VM and user experience are persistent. This means that the VM will likely be on and be updated, until the day it is destroyed for other reasons. Since the user profile and applications are by default contained within the VM, the user experience is persistent since they always access the same VM.

Deployment

Depending on the vendor's solution that you select, there are typically two primary ways to deploy persistent desktops. The first method of deploying persistent virtual desktops is to use the built in automated process that is part of the solution. This involves using a template VM that serves as the master or golden image from which all desktops for a pool will be created. The VDI broker software will create exact clones from the template that will be customized to have unique names after the cloning process is completed. They are they registered with the brokering software, and become available for use once a user is entitled to them.

Since this method is based on a master template, there must be one of these created and tested in advance. Depending on what and how many use cases you will be fulfilling with persistent desktops, you will likely need more than one template. Since the parameters for the template are fixed, they typically directly correlate to a use case and desktop pool.

If there are applications installed into the template, there is less of a chance that it can be used for multiple pools. Each of these templates can start form a single source that is your organizational standard, and includes all VDI tweaks made. Once it is customized for a use case, it becomes unique and must be managed accordingly.

This does save some time when you create a new image, but does nothing to lessen the operational burden of having a large amount of images. It is highly recommended to document the deployment of each master template. This includes all settings and changes made along with all software and applications installed along with versions. If you have to reverse engineer an image later, it will be a horrible and long process.

The second option for creating persistent desktops would be to use an existing well-defined process for deploying the desktop OS. This is probably the same process used to deploy OSs to physical devices. In this scenario, you would start out with a new empty VM and the deployment process would lay down the OS according to predefined settings. It would then follow on and deploy any applications directly into the VM afterwards. This process would be used whenever a new persistent virtual desktop is requested. The downside of this is that this is all done outside of the control of the VDI management and brokering software, which typically means that newly created desktops will have to be manually added to the pools before they are available to users.

Operations

Persistent virtual desktop management must also be considered. Each persistent virtual desktop is a separate VM, they start out identical and all become unique snowflakes once users begin to use them. These virtual desktops need to be managed using the same tools and techniques that are used for managing physical endpoints as the management is being shifted from the endpoint device itself to the VM in the data center.

If good desktop management procedures and tools are not in place, administrators will need to manually manage each desktop. This includes routine maintenance such as patching and application deployments and updates. If procedures and tools for effectively managing these, and other, tasks are not in place, administrators may be forced to manually log into each system to perform these tasks or impact the users by performing these tasks during business hours.

In simple terms, persistent full clone desktops are not providing the organization any operational benefit in the form of a reduction in effort or time.

It does likely reduce the time to provision new desktops, which may be enough of a benefit for some.

Infrastructure

Persistent desktops do not use any more or less host CPU or memory than their non-persistent counterparts. Since, however, they are all unique snowflakes, they do have different storage requirements. With each persistent desktop being a full copy of the template, this means that every desktop will require the same capacity as the template VM. If your template VM is provisioned for 50 GB of disk capacity and is consuming 30 GB of space, you can roughly calculate needed storage capacity by multiplying by the number of virtual desktops.

Since persistent desktops are typically comprised of a single virtual disk, the storage design is fairly straightforward. You will follow the recommendations from the EUC vendor on the density of number of VM per storage volume. Since it is a single virtual disk, you will not need to worry about placing different volumes on different performing storage volumes.

Disk capacity is a primary concern, and you should choose a storage solution that supports intelligent cloning, deduplication and compression, if available. This will reduce the amount of storage required and/or allocated for supporting the virtual desktop environment by reducing the number of duplicate blocks written to storage. This will enable you to place more desktops on the storage solution. Designing and sizing infrastructure is covered in more detail in Chapter 15.

Also to be considered is backup and high availability. Since persistent desktops are full virtual desktops, the user is usually as tightly coupled to the VM, as they were to their physical endpoint device. This means that each persistent VM or at minimum the user data must be able to be restored at the remote site or protected by replicating to the secondary site. This will ensure that users will be able to work in the event of an outage to their personal virtual desktop. Data protection and disaster recovery is covered in more detail in Chapter 12.

Use Cases

Persistent full clone desktops could be used for almost any use case, and are often selected because they are familiar and easy for most admins. It is also an easy migration path since there is little change in the environment. In reality, there are fewer reasons to use them than in the past. The most suitable targets for persistent desktops are still developer use cases, and when users need to self-install applications. Outside of those two uses cases, if there is an application that is licensed against the computer hardware, they are ideal since the application and user are tied to the same virtual desktop.

Non-Persistent Desktops

Unlike their persistent desktop counterparts, a non-persistent desktop implies that changes are scrapped after each session. This is very different from the desktop and laptop computers that are deployed to office workers.

In the past, physical desktops tools like Windows Steady State and Deep Freeze would have been used in places like computer labs and public access kiosks to prevent users from making changes to machines. Any changes that the user does make, such as installing an application or changing the desktop background, are written to a temporary place on the hard drive. When the user logs out or reboots, that temporary file is removed, and the system reverts to a known good configuration.

Non-persistent desktops generally work on the same principle. Changes are written to a delta disk or temporary file, and when the user logs out, the machine is shut down and the temporary disk is removed or the desktop is deleted and recreated. Unless it is redirected, the user's profile and application settings would be lost when the desktop is reverted to a known good state. A user profile management solution is required when using non-persistent desktops.

58 | *Architecting EUC Solutions*

User Data — User profile and files.

Applications — Applications presented or layered.

Delta Disk — Captures all writes from user session.

Gold Image — R/O OS image for all desktops.

OS Disk — Read only fed from the golden image.

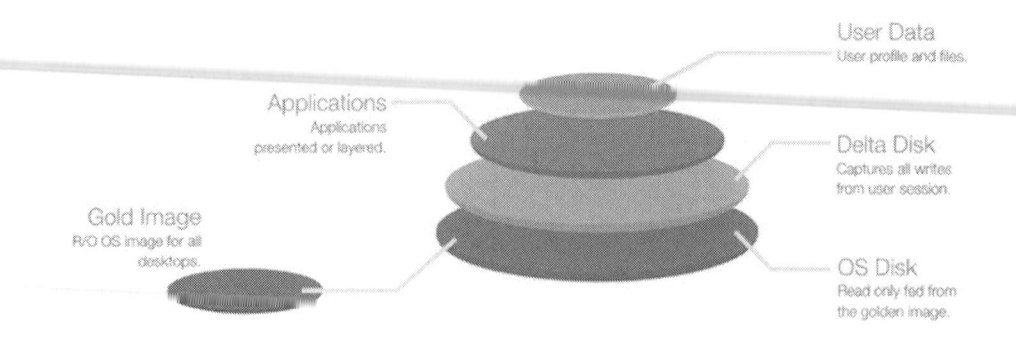

Non-Persistent Desktops

Users are generally not able to install their own applications on non-persistent desktops. The virtual desktop team is responsible for managing applications, and any application must either be embedded in the gold image or presented form a host server or via an application layer. Application management alternatives are discussed in greater detail in Chapter 9. Tools like SCCM or Mirage can be used to manage the gold images. They are not very effective at managing non-persistent desktops once they are deployed, though.

Deployment

Non-persistent desktops are created by the VDI brokering software. There are popular methods from VMware and Citrix that are most commonly deployed. They are VMware Linked clones, Citrix Provisioning Services (PVS) and Citrix Machine Creation Services (MCS). These solutions are ideally suited for non-persistent desktops, as they are easily reverted to a known good state.

VMware Linked Clones

Linked clones are VMs that share or reference the same set of disks. These are commonly referred to as the master or golden images. With linked clones, the master image is known as the replica disk. Read IO is served up from the shared disks, and all writes are redirected to a delta or change disk for that VM.

Linked Clones are non-persistent by nature, but the user experience can be made to feel persistent with the use of profile management discussed in Chapter 10 and efficient application management discussed in Chapter 9. While this section is focused on linked clones from VMware, Citrix also offers Machine Creation Services (MCS), which is nearly identical to what VMware offers. The majority of the content following also applies to MCS.

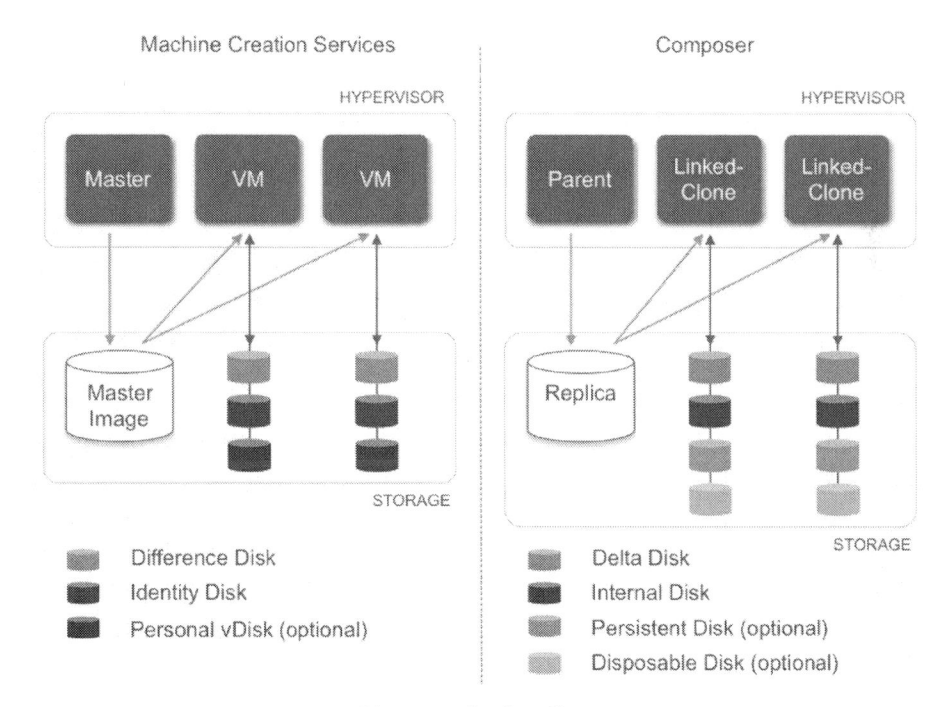

```
Machine Creation Services                    Composer

              HYPERVISOR                              HYPERVISOR
   Master    VM    VM                    Parent   Linked-   Linked-
                                                   Clone     Clone

   Master                                  Replica
   Image
                              STORAGE
                                                              STORAGE
   ■ Difference Disk                      ■ Delta Disk
   ■ Identity Disk                        ■ Internal Disk
   ■ Personal vDisk (optional)            ▨ Persistent Disk (optional)
                                          ▨ Disposable Disk (optional)
```

Photo credited to Citrix

Operations – Linked Clones

There are some operational benefits to using desktops based on Linked Clones. The first benefit is that they provide a single point of management. New applications and updates only need to be installed in one place – the golden image. Once the updates are installed, they can be pushed to a single desktop, a subset of desktops or all of the desktops in the pool that uses the updated golden image. This is done by changing the read only virtual disk image that these VMs use. This can significantly lighten the administrative overhead for managing virtual desktops.

Another benefit of using linked clones is that it is easy to roll back a VM to a known good state. If a linked-clone desktop suffers an error such as a blue screen – or it gets infected by malware, an administrator can quickly revert that VM back to the known good state and get the user back up and running quickly. That user is not waiting for someone from IT to diagnose the issue, clean the malware, or rebuild their PC.

One nice benefit of linked clone technology is that they often provide their own form of version control. VMware Horizon Composer and Citrix MCS both utilize snapshots of the target machine. These snapshots are utilized when creating the reference disks that the linked clone desktops will use as the golden image. Administrators can easily roll back changes on the golden images if there is a mistake without having to rebuild them from scratch. It is important to note that desktops will need to be recomposed or redeployed if a base image with an error was deployed into production. A recompose operation is when the golden image is changed or a different snapshot on the golden image is selected, thus changing the version that the pool is using as the read only copy. This requires a reboot of all desktops in the pool at once or on a staggered schedule.

There are some drawbacks to deploying Linked Clone virtual desktops. The process of changing out the linked clone base image can be time consuming, especially if there are a lot of virtual desktops that need to be updated. This typically restricts recompose update operations to off-hours.

There are three other potential drawbacks to virtual desktops based on Linked Clones:
- The first issue is master image and pool sprawl. Master image sprawl is when multiple linked clone master or golden images are created to address use case application requirements. An example of this would be to create a master image and a pool for each use case to address each cases application requirements. This increases management overhead because there are more images and pools that need to be updated, monitored, and managed. Too save on the need to have multiple master

images, different application management alternatives are discussed in Chapter 9 that offer different presentation and layering options to alleviate this sprawl.
- The second potential drawback involves ensuring a consistent user environment on all workstations. Many non-persistent virtual desktop environments utilize linked clones, and these desktops are discarded or reverted to a known good state when the user logs off. Any customizations or changes that the user made will be lost at that time. The user's settings need to be roamed or migrated with them between desktops to ensure a consistent user experience. Some applications, such as Lotus Notes, do not work well, even when user settings are roamed, and additional steps might be required to make sure that all user applications work as expected. Capturing and managing user profiles is discussed in detail in Chapter 10. However, there may be use cases that you would not want to persistent user changes and profiles. This allows non-persistent desktops to easily provide this without any additional layers.
- The third drawback of using linked clone desktops is that there needs to be a well-documented practice for managing and updating the virtual desktop golden images. Since linked clone desktops utilize the same base disk, any errors, mistakes or bad updates could potentially impact hundreds or thousands of users. It may not be possible to fix the issues that users encounter without some form of downtime. If the design calls for using a significant number of linked clone desktops, the administrators responsible for handling updates to the virtual desktops should consider creating a test and acceptance plan for any changes, and get user sign-off before deploying the updated desktop images.

Infrastructure – Linked Clones

Linked clones typically provide storage capacity savings, since they typically use less storage than persistent full clone desktops. Since each linked clone desktop in a pool references the same golden image, many files that all desktops would have, such as the core operating system and application files, are only stored once in the golden image. This results in each non-persistent desktop not needing to store copies of all the shared data, and only needs a few gigabytes of temporary space for the disposable writes to be stored during the user's session.

Historically, the linked clone non-persistent desktops had very different storage performance requirements than persistent desktops. This has driven by the fact that the entire pool of desktops, which could be hundreds or more, are all reading from the golden image. Especially at busy times such as logins, reboots, updates, this caused a high spike in storage performance needs. If the storage was not able to fulfill all the requests the users experience suffered greatly.

In the past, storage architectures tried to use different tiers of storage to place the golden image on faster storage, such as all flash or 15K drives. The delta disks and other portions were placed on mid-level storage tiers. This architecture only provided additional complexity to the environment, and most often was unable to supply the required performance unless the storage was oversized to start.

Today, with the advent of modern storage architectures that intelligently use hybrid disk and flash or all-flash storage, these performance concerns are all gone. By selecting one of these modern storage architectures, which are discussed further in Chapter 15, the complexity and performance problems are solved. There is no longer a need to separate the different disk parts of a non-persistent solution onto different storage tiers or solutions.

Citrix Provisioning Server

One unique virtual desktop deployment method that is only available in Citrix environments is called Citrix Provisioning Server (PVS). It essentially boots and streams the required bits and files from the golden image over the network.

In a Citrix PVS design, there are typically multiple PVS servers at each site that you will be hosting desktop infrastructure. For example, you might have two data centers with compute and storage infrastructure for virtual desktops. Each of these sites would have a highly available PVS design that included multiple PVS servers. The final number would be driven by the number of PVS targets that would be booting from the servers.

PVS designs differ from Linked Clones because the PVS servers are the point that caches the golden Image and streams it to all PVS targets- in this case, the virtual desktops. The non-persistent part is similar to Linked Clones- just that the read only golden image comes from PVS servers rather than a shared virtual disk on the storage system. All of the non-persistent desktops still require a temp delta disks to write changes to that are discarded upon reboots.

Operations – PVS Desktops

In many ways, desktops managed by Citrix PVS share many of the operational strengths and weaknesses as linked clones. They both rely on a golden image that is updated when the image is patched or receives application updates. You will suffer the same golden image sprawl challenges if you intend on installing use cases applications in your images. Creating silos for use cases that create pools of desktops with specific changes would require separate images. There is additional risk with PVS over linked clones from an operation perspective, as there are many opportunities where small errors could immediately impact users

With PVS, when an image is updated the process is a bit lighter weight and faster. Since you are not completely destroying the VM each time and doing multiple storage and vCenter Server related tasks. The process is a reboot of the PVS target that upon reboot will be streaming the newly updated golden image.

Infrastructure – PVS Desktops

Since PVS based desktops are streamed, the first thing of note is that the large surge of read-only storage performance requirement is greatly reduced. This is because, if sized correctly, the PVS servers are able to completely cache the golden image into the memory of the PVS servers. This allows the surge of read traffic from the gold master to be performed in server memory, and not be sent to the storage solution. PVS offers similar space efficiency as linked clones due to the nature of a having a single gold master image or a single image per pool.

PVS then offers several options on how the delta disk for writes created during users' sessions can be architected. The first option would be the same as linked clones, PVS can also use a virtual disk file that would be placed on the storage solution for each PVS desktop. These virtual disk files would all write to the desktop's delta disk. This would rely on the storage solution to provide the capacity and performance required for all write traffic.

There are two other options that include using host memory as a place to use for this write traffic. The first option is to use host memory for all writes and is called Write Cache. This correlates to providing each PVS desktop with additional RAM memory that is used for writes. The performance of this alternative is very impressive and removes nearly all demand from your storage solution. The downside of this is that, if sized improperly and if desktops are not rebooted on a schedule, the desktops will crash once the RAM based write buffer is filled up.

The third option is a combination of the first two. It uses RAM memory for write caching, but allows it to overflow into a virtual disk on the storage solution if memory fills up. While there is a lot of debate on whether to cache writes in memory or disk, for PVS architects if sized right the performance of either will be excellent. With today's modern storage architectures discussed in Chapter 15, there is little concern about using storage for caching.

Use Cases – Non-Persistent Desktops

Non-Persistent desktops could be used for almost any use case, but historically were a challenge to most because the need to manage user profiles and applications differently than what was traditionally done. Non-persistent desktops were only suited for environments where all users would require the same application load, or when storage was a serious constraint. It was possible to utilize non-persistent desktops for other use cases, but it would require creating additional desktop images and pools for different application loads. The advent of desktop layering solutions and application presentation has made linked clone desktops suitable for most use cases.

Today non-persistent desktops should be the preferred method and only ruled out when the requirements cannot be met. This means that most use cases outside of developer use cases and when users need to self-install applications should go on non-persistent desktops. These two use cases can be done on non-persistent desktops, but the additional challenges to meet the needs of these two use cases are not always worth the additional complexity.

Dedicated vs. Pooled Non-Persistent Desktops

There are two ways to assign non-persistent desktops to users. The first way is to dedicate specific desktops to users. This is similar to how persistent desktops are assigned, and the user will get the same machine every time they log in. Unlike persistent desktops, a dedicated non-persistent desktop will periodically be reset to a known-good configuration. This can be as frequently as every log-off or during a maintenance period where the desktop gold image is updated after patching or installing new applications.

Dedicated non-persistent desktops are good for when you want to provide the benefits of non-persistent desktops, such as refreshing the machine to a known-good state on logoff, while providing applications that require the user to have the same machine every time.

The other way to assign non-persistent desktops is known as the pooled method. The pooled method assigns a desktop to each user every time they log in. When the user is logs out, the desktop is returned to the pool where it can be assigned to another user. The user is not guaranteed to have the same desktop every time they log in. In fact, they will usually have a different desktop on each login. You will want to consider using a tool like BGInfo to display the computer name on the desktop so they can easily provide it when contacting their help desk for support.

Shared Hosted Desktops

Shared Hosted desktops are more commonly referred to as Remote Desktop Session Host (RDSH), if you are old-school IT they were called Terminal Services previously. These desktops are servers that are configured so that multiple users can log in at the same time to access a desktop, applications, and other resources. Each user receives a session that looks similar to a Windows Desktop, but users are unable to install their own applications as the servers that host the sessions are centrally managed by a dedicated administrator or team.

Since a number of users are sharing the same server OS, the resources of the RDSH server are shared amongst the sessions. While RDSH has come a long way since original Terminal Services, there still can be some level of resource content between sessions. Also if an application on a server begins to behave badly, all the sessions on that server will be negatively affects.

Shared desktops do not provide the same level of separation that virtual desktops offer with each desktop having its own discrete OS running. Since all sessions are sharing the same OS, files system, and registry, there is not the same level of security isolation that VDI provides. If you have use cases that can live within these constraints, they may be an ideal fit for shared hosted desktops.

Shared hosted desktop technology is available natively from Microsoft and third party vendors such as Citrix XenApp, VMware Horizon, and Dell vWorkspace, as they use RDSH as the base for their solutions.

Because most environments utilize multiple servers to provide shared desktop services and load balancers to distribute connections, a profile management solution is required to ensure that the user's environment and application settings are available on all servers.

Operations – Shared Hosted Desktops

The operational story for shared hosted desktops is someplace in the middle of what persistent and non-persistent desktops offer. You are going to be managing RDSH servers, which may be full OS deployments. You can, however, use Citrix PVS or MCS also for the session hosts.

Where you will get the operational benefits is from the fact that there will be far fewer session hosts to manage than persistent desktops. With an average of 20-50 desktop sessions per RDSH server the number of VMs being managed is greatly reduced.

Infrastructure – Shared Hosted Desktops

The infrastructure for the RDSH servers will also be similar to a scaled down persistent desktop environment. The storage capacity and performance requirements will be greatly reduced also since there are far fewer instances created and running. By having far less VMs performing intensive storage tasks the I/O requirements are much lower. With dozens of users per server VM, the impact of reboots and patching exercises are far less extensive than having a VM for each user.

3D Graphics Accelerations

If you look at the specs for your computer, you will see that it has hardware dedicated to processing video and 3D graphics. Some applications can even take advantage of this hardware to offload some tasks from the system's CPUs or require it due to work with high-end graphics.

Until recently, 3D acceleration was not an option for virtual desktops or servers running the RDSH role, and applications that utilized discrete graphics processing unit (GPU) card would experience decreased performance or be unable to run.

New technologies and techniques have allowed 3D acceleration within virtual EUC environments. Some of these technologies are:

- Dedicated (Pass-Thru) 3D Acceleration – a GPU is installed in the server and passed through to a VM. The VM has full access to the GPU and can utilize all of its features.
- NVIDIA GRID vGPU – This technology, which is available on Citrix XenServer and VMware vSphere, allows VMs to share access to GPU resources on an NVIDIA GRID card.

There are some drawbacks to the current 3D acceleration technologies. These include:

- Cost – 3D acceleration supports a limited number of high-end professional cards from NVIDIA and AMD. These cards are significantly more expensive than the cards that are usually found in workstations. The cost can typically be justified for high-end use cases, but not others.
- User to Host Density Limits – 3D cards can only support a limited number of users per host, and this can increase the number of hosts, and costs, required to support the environment.

- Limited Support for High Availability – Depending on the 3D acceleration technology used, virtual desktops and RDSH servers with 3D GPU cards may not be able to live migrate. If a GPU is dedicated to a VM, it can only start up and run on the specific host that has its GPU. VMs using NVIDIA GRID vGPU can start up and run on other hosts, but they cannot live migrate.

Even with these drawbacks, there are still some use cases that greatly benefit from having a 3D graphics card. These use cases include:

- CAD/CAM/Building Information Modelling (BIM)
- Medical Imaging
- 3D Animation and Rendering
- Video Editing

There are other applications that can also benefit from having GPU support, but typically cannot justify the additional expense. The following are a couple examples of everyday apps that can benefit from GPU's.

- Office 2013
- Internet Explorer

Summary

If designed properly virtual desktops can provide great operational benefits, by reducing the level of effort while increasing your organizations ability to react and provision faster. The alternatives discussed in this chapter illustrate a number of different approaches to meeting these goals while still satisfying the requirements of your use cases.

[7]
Physical PCs and Laptops

At this point in the book, virtual desktops have already been covered in depth, and in Chapter 9 the book will cover application management., There still are, however, and will be physical device requirements within your environment. The physical PC and laptop will have a place in your environment for years to come. Whether you have use cases for them or allow users to bring their own device (BYOD), they will be present and you need to have options for managing them when appropriate.

For the purpose of this chapter's topic, it will be focusing on physical devices that run a fully featured OS. The primary OS used in most organizations is a Microsoft Windows based client version. This could be Windows 7, 8, and 10 will be available by the time this book is published. You may even still run into pockets of Windows XP usage. There is an increase amount of adoption and demand for Apple Mac OS based devices within organizations, and some organizations in specific industries will be using a Linux OS on their devices.
This chapter will focus on solutions based on Windows based OS, but many of the same challenges exist across OSs. This chapter is preparing you to understand what your goals will likely be and how to better identify and evaluate your options.

The Challenge

How will you know when to manage physical devices and when not to? A typical stance on this topic is if the device is company owned and provided, you will be required to and will want to manage the device. The focus in this chapter is around managing the OS of these PCs and laptops. These are mostly Windows-based and are the most labor intensive. Apple computers, though, are increasingly popular devices for business users, and most organizations lack the tools to manage Macs.

The tools available for organizations to manage Apple devices are still very limited and not well known to many teams. You will have to do some research to see what is available, and how well they might meet your requirements. Will you be looking for something that can push out OS updates to a large collection of devices without just asking them to update themselves? You may also be interested in any imaging features to help deploy your base image. Perhaps you want the ability to purchase applications in large quantities from the app store and assign to devices is a popular request. These are all things to consider managing for your Apple users.

When it comes to Windows devices, teams a primarily focused on deploying builds, re-imaging devices, and installing Windows updates. These are all tasks that desktop admins love to perform (insert sarcasm here). While these are not fun tasks, they are still necessary and important. The processes for these tasks have been around for a long time, and little has changed. There are a number of tools available for doing these tasks. There are still many organizations that use Microsoft System Center Configuration Manager (SCCM), Altiris and ZENworks. The problem is these tools have not changed their methods in more than a decade.

If your organization has these processes down to a science and spends little time on them, then you may not need to worry about improving them. But if you support a large number of desktops and have a team that spends their days working on these tasks, then you should also explore new options to improve these tasks.

The Desired State

Most believe that the legacy approach of imaging physical PCs is way past its expiration date and needs some fresh thinking. The goal is to be able to take an approach similar to what you can in the virtual desktop architecture. You would like to be able to prepare a single image per Windows version, and be able to use it throughout your environment. This single image can be updated with routine patches each month, and then the updates would be distributed to all endpoints under management through the image update.

This can be a challenge since typically physical endpoints must boot and run off of a locally installed OS. They cannot be created or destroyed as easily as virtual desktops can. Also, many organizations do not backup or mange the user profiles on these physical devices, so there is data that cannot be destroyed or lost. A physical device also has device drivers that are unique to each brand and model of device with which must be accounted for, since most organizations have a wide range of models under management. Dividing a device into OS, user and application layers for easier management and updates is not easy. While you do research and evaluate options for making this process better, pay close attention to how the product deals with these constraints.

74 | *Architecting EUC Solutions*

[Diagram showing layers: App 1, App 2, App 3, App 4 / User Profile / Windows Operating System / Physical Device Drivers]

While this book is not focused on any specify vendor products, current feedback is that VMware Mirage is making a significant impact in the deployment, management, and upgrading of Windows OS. Mirage brings single image management to physical Windows devices by its use of layering technology. Mirage allows a single corporate Windows image to be created per OS version. Then through its layering technology, Mirage can layer on device drivers and applications, while identifying and backing up user data. This allows for image update to be sent out to any devices when the main image is patched, while only sending the changes out in a single push of data.

While exploring this need within your design spend some time and learn how Mirage may help with your Windows management.

Use Cases

The previous chapter sections just covered some of the important details about what you would be managing with physical devices in your design. The remainder of the chapter will talk through some of the reasons that you may need or want to use physical PCs or laptops in some of your use cases.

Rich Endpoints

A rich endpoint is a device that has a full OS that is installed on it. These are typically Windows devices or thin clients with an embedded version of Windows. They can also be Apple or Linux devices in some cases.

There are a few reasons that organizations would choose to use a rich endpoint. One of the leading reasons is that they already own them. They do not wish to just toss out these devices that are already owned or might lease only to incur additional expense. The desire is to repurpose them in some fashion that allows them to be the device that is primarily used to access the new EUC services. Likely there is very little or no work performed directly on these endpoints. A common direction is to re-image them and lock them down for the primary purpose of running the client to access your new services.

Another important reason to use a rich endpoint is to take advantage of its local resources. Depending on the vendor that you select, they may offer the ability to utilize local resources to improve performance of the end-user's experience. This could be something like redirecting flash to a local web browser to improve the performance. There have been several features within vendors' client software that has offered features that require a rich endpoint of which you can take advantage. Once you understand what the client from your selected vendor offers, you can use those detail in your endpoint selection process.

Power Users

A small number of users or use cases may still require the resources of a workstation class computer to perform their job or specific functions. These types of situations are still commonly addressed by having them continue to use a local device. While centralized virtual desktops has continually improved over the years and virtualized graphics (vGPU) is getting close to mainstream, there can still be a significant cost associated with servicing these users versus your other use cases.

The primary decision here is will this use case remain a physical device or be centralized. Then you will need to decide if there is a way that you can improve the management options and reduce effort for these devices, or if they will remain business as usual. The legacy method for these devices was described earlier in the chapter that would involve the initial OS deployment or imaging. Then the ongoing monthly patching efforts that must be kept maintained.

The real opportunity here is that these are likely to remain physical devices, is can one use something like VMware Mirage, or another tool, to greatly reduce the operational effort for managing them. If this can be accomplished, then you should not be worried about leaving them as physical devices, as it may be a more cost effective solution. Also, if the use case does not require mobility or other benefits that a centralized solution may provide, remaining physical holds as the right choice.

Bring Your Own Device

Newsflash: people like to pick and use their own devices, whether it is a phone, tablet, or laptop. Some do it because they like the look, others for status, while others do it to meet their personal requirements. Regardless of the reasons, users are increasingly demanding the opportunities to use more of their personal devices to perform work related duties. This topic will be discussed through several chapters of the book.

With regards to personal devices as it relates to physical devices, these are owned by the end users, so they are not going to be interested in their employer managing their devices. They do not want work policies applied to private areas and data. The trick here is to walk the thin line that exists between these two worlds. You will be required to provide access, but maintain security and compliance.

One option for this if they require a full desktop experience is to deposit a VM on their personal computer. This VM will run locally and consume local resources. This would allow them to work in a connected or disconnected mode. The organizations data may or may not be allowed to be stored within these VMs. If there is data, or even if not, you will want to explore your options for securing these locally executed VMs.

The ability to deploy, manage, and secure the VMs will be key to supporting this type of use case. This approach allows you to provide a company managed desktop to these users while allowing them to use their personal devices. There will be minimal requirements for their devices to run their installed operating system and a managed VM. This will have to be qualified and marketed as part of the service offering.

Controlling the security of these VMs through policies will be critical for success. You will need to have a way to enable and disable access. Ability to set policy to choose whether you will allow such things as copy and paste or the ability to mount USB devices to the VM. Lastly, there must be a method that allows the VM to be deleted or a poison pill approach that disables the VM when the users access should be removed. These policies must be able to be controlled remotely to be effective.

Offline Use Cases

In the past years of VDI, the industry has seen multiple vendors try and solve the offline use cases by allowing users to check out their virtual desktop when they needed to be disconnected. This was a time and bandwidth consuming exercise that no one liked. The vendors have finally figured out that the check-out approach is flawed and have even removed the option from the products for the most part.

The need for some users to work disconnected can be a legitimate requirement; the key is to figuring out exactly what they will need to use while disconnected is important. If they will only use productivity apps is this state because all enterprise apps require a connection to the data center, this may change your approach.

This use case is not that different than the previously discussed power user, except these users are using a laptop for the endpoint and most likely to not require a workstation based laptop.

Summary

The delicate balance to watch for with physical devices is to accomplish your goals whether it is a better user experience or to save costs. Be mindful, though, as to not increase your workload. If you use a rich endpoint as your device for a group of users to access virtual desktops, understand that VDI is going to be providing you a new set of features and benefits. By keeping the rich endpoint you are now potentially managing two copies of Windows for each user as an example.

For this reason alone, it is worth exploring new methods and tools for managing these devices to reduce your support efforts. While this book could not cover every use case for a physical device, hopefully the samples provided here are enough for one to understand the thought process and understand the challenges and opportunities available.

[8]
Desktop as a Service

This chapter is going to take a look at Desktop as a Service (DaaS) and find out what it has to offer, along with how it may or may not fit into your EUC design. First, you have to cover what exactly DaaS means. In very simple terms, DaaS is the idea that you pay a per-user cost and get a virtual desktop from a cloud or hosting provider. The per-user pricing is generally based on a monthly fee that can be negotiated based upon the length of your agreement and the features that you are purchasing. Almost every DaaS provider is going to be offering different desktop sizes that range from a small version that will satisfy many common use cases to a large high performing desktop for the power users. These desktop sizes will also drive the user pricing along with previous mentioned factors.

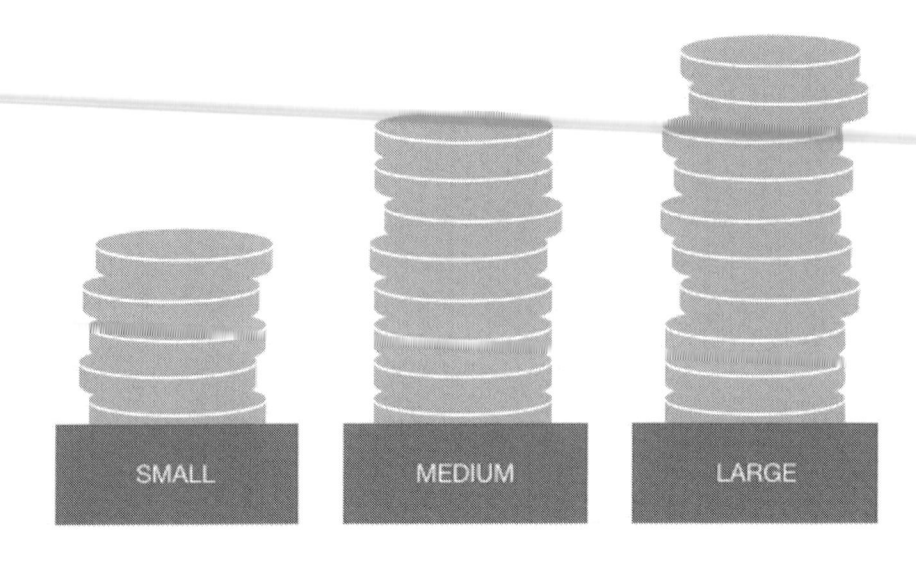

DaaS Desktop Costs

The services that each DaaS provider might offer can vary wildly along with costs, but the idea is similar. You show up with your 200 users, and you pay a fixed rate per user with the hope that there is little that you have to do other than consume the desktops. The rest of this chapter will take a look at how realistic the idea of DaaS is, and what are some of the use cases that might make the most sense.

DaaS Pros

When you hear a sales pitch for DaaS it reminds me a little bit of those California tourism commercials. The ones where the weather is awesome, everyone is beautiful, and they do not mention crippling debt or water issues that California faces. DaaS has a lot of appeal to organizations that have been interested in VDI in the past. Some like to think of DaaS as VDI in the cloud, all the benefits, fixed pricing and without all the hard work.

Like California tourism, DaaS does have a lot of benefits to consider. A list of the benefits was compiled with a brief commentary on each one. There are still many more to consider but these are ones that were at the top of the list.

- **Established cost structure** - Much different than building your own VDI design, the cost of DaaS is fixed. Organizations know exactly what the cost per user will be. This paints a clear picture when scaling the number of users.
- **Quick to start** - Much like other software offerings there is a very short period between swiping your credit card to the moment you can begin consuming the service. Given DaaS is probably a bit longer than singling up for something like Evernote, but far faster than purchasing and building your own infrastructure.
- **Nothing to build** - You are purchasing a service; there should be nothing for you to build. The desktop hosting infrastructure is provided by the vendor and all you have to do is move users in.
- **Easy to try out** - Since there is nothing to build like on-premises deployments, organizations can easily sign up for a trial of a small number of users. Put the service through different tests to ensure that it will meet your requirements without a large investment of capital or time.
- **Cheap to start out** - With the primary costs being a per user fee. There is not the same large capital spends there would be with building an on-premises solution.
- **Remote locations** - This might be the most attractive benefit in most people's eyes. Most DaaS providers can or will be able to offer data center locations in different regions around the world. It enables the offering of desktops that are closer in proximity to different user groups versus running from a single centrally located site.

DaaS Cons

Now that the benefits of DaaS have been covered, this chapter will cover some of the cons. It is definitely not a California commercial here, maybe a bit more like a South Dakota advertisement. Looks like a beautiful place to visit, but there is a reason that the population density is one of the lowest in the country.

The following drawbacks being covered are not the nail in the coffin for DaaS. Depending on your organization and the requirements of your use cases these points may not be as important to you as the next person.

- **Provider service level agreements (SLAs)** - As you shop around for DaaS, providers can you find one that publishes detailed SLA metrics that would meet your requirements. What if you seek a higher level of availability then a provider offers by default, can you negotiate with them? Determining SLAs can be a difficult and lengthy process.
- **Application access** - If the desktops are at the DaaS provider, your applications are likely in your on-premises data center. How will the application perform with the added latency when accessed remotely?
- **Application flexibility** – What apps can be installed and how should one proceed?
- **Data location** - Depending on how things are architected, you will be or have a high likelihood of corporate data being stored in the cloud. This may be an issue for some. Just realize users are going to store data on their desktops, and by default they will be at the hosting provider.
- **Flexibility** - This will vary based on providers likely and the size of your request, but you will probably find that providers will be only so flexible. They cannot meet the requests from every customer and may have to say no to most requests to keep a standardized environment.
- **Limited OS support** - You are likely to be presented with a limited set of Windows OS choices. This will vary some from provider to provider. Some may only offer server bases operating systems (2008 & 2012). While others will offer server and client operating systems (Windows 7 and 8). The client OS deployments will need to be on

dedicated hardware for each customer for licensing reasons, and that may affect your pricing or the quantity in which you can purchase.
- **Microsoft licensing** - You are now running OS and potentially business apps in a provider's data center. Does your current licensing model help you with this? Can you purchase the licensing as part of the service or is this going to be an added expense?
- **Network bandwidth** - Connecting to cloud services is just something that is normal and IT organizations will have to get comfortable with this. DaaS offers a bigger challenge here, because these are desktop sessions that can consume far more bandwidth than your typical SaaS application. A user is not going to be consuming 300K to 2Mbs over the course of a full workday on services like Box.net or Salesforce, but they could easily with a desktop in the cloud. This can be more painful if they are connecting from multiple devices during the day. All of this adds up to be a large amount of bandwidth that would not be consume for an on-premises solution.
- **Exit strategy** – A cloud exit strategy is a very important thing to consider when you are taking any workload to the cloud. Think about what you would do if you want out of the DaaS solution.

DaaS Questions

Along with all the advantages and drawbacks that DaaS brings to the conversation, there are still going to be unanswered questions. To this point the book has assembled a list of questions that were at top of mind when discussing DaaS. There will certainly be many others that come up that pertain to your organization and its requirements.

What is the provider willing to talk about in how they secure their DaaS environment for each customer? As a business entity one will need to know how the organization's data and networks will be protected from other DaaS customers and external threats. Also, what if the organization has specific PCI,

HIPAA, or other regulatory requirements that must be met? How will they help or prevent us from meeting these regulations?

What will the connectivity options be for each provider that is evaluated? Will they have a single method or be able to offer multiple methods? Common choices would be some type of VPN connection between the provider data center and the customer's data center. Do they offer any type of direct connectivity option? Can one order a circuit and have it terminated at their site to create a private connection between the data centers without the need for a VPN connection? Each customer is likely to have a preference in what option they would choose and this may affect your choice when evaluating providers.

What most organizations need from a DaaS service is far more than just a desktop to log into. Does the provider manage anything other than the infrastructure below the service? Do they manage anything from the OS up? If they provide any of these services, how much does that affect the per desktop pricing? Or do these types of tasks fall back to the customer? If so, then just renting a desktop may not be that attractive. The following is a short list of one time and ongoing tasks that would be needed by most customers that are missed in most DaaS offerings, or at least must be further investigated.

- **OS Patching** - How is this done and who does it? Simply turning on auto-update in Windows is not the answer that one would want to hear.
- **Printers** - How will printing be managed in DaaS? Does it work like it does today or will this architecture present new challenges?
- **User Files** - Where will the users store their data? Will it be on each desktop, will there be file servers at the DaaS provider? Can or should one be mapping drives to shares back in the data center?
- **Applications** - How will applications be presented and managed in this environment? Do they offer anything to ease this burden? Does this work all fallback to the customer?
- **Authentication** - What will the options be for user authentication? Do they allow a customer to place a domain controller in your DaaS setup

and do you want to? Do they only provide an authentication model that cannot be federated with your internal source?
- **New user setup** - Today you likely have a defined process for the desktop setup process for a new user. Likely things are automatically created and the users Outlook client is auto configured when they login. Will you be able to re-use some or all of these processes in the DaaS environment?
- **Backups** - You will be very interested in what providers are backing up and what they are not. Also consider how often these backups taking place. Does this meet your organization's requirements? Would your users have the ability to restore their data themselves?

Another thing to discuss with DaaS vendors as you evaluate what is available in the market is what happens when you want to leave their service? This might be one of the last questions organizations think of when signing up with a new vendor, but in today's cloud-based world, it should be one of the first on the list. You will need to understand how your data is handled and deleted when you exit.

What about those backups that they have been taking over the time you used their service? Will they be able to provide you with copies or exports of that data? Will they delete those backups? How will they be able to provide proof of the data being purged?

Use Cases

After carefully evaluating all of the benefits and drawbacks of DaaS, you should be getting an idea of what use cases might be candidates for DaaS. There will likely be some use cases that you could force into a DaaS model, provided that you can make some compromises. The recommendation is to use DaaS in your EUC offering and qualify use cases for it rather than trying to find a reason to use it.

There are a few common use cases that are better candidates for using DaaS. The requirements of these may vary between organizations but the core needs are usually similar. A short list of these is provided below with basic details.

- **Short-Term Projects** - You may have short-term surges in demand for desktop services. These requests do not last long and are not always easily planned for. Depending on the applications requirements, this type of request may be a great fit for DaaS. You can quickly request capacity and depending on your contract, turn back in the resources when the project is complete.
- **Offshore Developers** - This type of use case has been seen at several customers. The developers do not have a requirement for a performant connection to backend infrastructure in your data center. They primarily write code in the desktop, but your organization wants to maintain ownership of the intellectual property. With this approach you are able to purchase desktop capacity in a region that is located close to the resources that will be performing the work, thus giving them a better user experience.
- **Student Labs** - The requirements for these types of labs vary greatly, so take this one with a grain of salt. These labs can be a bit like the short-term projects use case. They had a relatively short life span and can be disposed of when complete. Depending the number of students that sign up for a time period the demand can vary greatly.

Summary

In summary the status of DaaS is still rather immature today, but will continue to improve over the coming years to be a more valuable service. As vendors improve the tools that provide DaaS, with increased customer interest, and as partners also mature, their DaaS supporting services the demand for DaaS will also increase. This will be a good space to watch and see how they will expand their ability to provide additional use cases for organizations.

[9]
Application Management

When it comes to EUC designs and projects, the application is typically the King. The end users do not care what type of infrastructure you are hosting the application or desktop on, or what physical location they are hosted in. They want or need access to applications, and want them to be highly available with good performance. These are their basic needs, there may be a number of other needs or requirements that build upon this, most of which will be discussed through the chapter.

The application need on the professional side is driven by the end users' requirements to get their jobs done. Most roles require applications to enter, modify, report, or create data. For this, they need to use applications to complete their daily tasks or generate revenue. On the personal side, applications are what people want to use to consume information or be entertained. This has become very apparent in the age of tablets and smartphones. The world saw Apple dominate this by having the best app store that offered the most complete set of quality applications. Other vendors lagged behind while they worked on their user experience and tried to attract more developers. Sure, the devices mattered in this race too, but having a cool device and few apps has not worked out well for several companies.

This brings up the phrase: "Applications can make or break your project." If you cannot provide applications to users in the methods that make them easy to consume and be highly available, the project is doomed to fail. Failing to deliver key applications will seriously constrain the use cases that can be delivered or delivering a key application with too many restrictions will both have adverse effects. In the end, the end users are either going to use a company provide device or BYOD, either way, they will need to use applications. You should be providing them access that can accommodate the different use cases and access methods that were identified in your requirements gathering phase.

A sticking point that has conflicted many of customers is that they do not see a single method of managing applications for both their new virtual environments and the legacy physical environments. The chances of being able to select a single application management approach and use it in both environments is minimal. If you do, then you will likely be making large sacrifices to flexibility or adding costs in one of the environments. You need to get past this point early. What you do in the virtual environment does not need to mirror what you have done with desktops for the last decade. There are, however, opportunities to share some tools or approaches between the two, but there are going to be differences. This will be covered in the application management sections in the remaining parts of this chapter.

Why is it Called Application Management?

This is a great question. In the past it has been called many things and when it came to EUC projects, like what is being covered in this book it was called application presentation because you are typically presenting applications to users. While many of the names are fine, they can be misleading or do not cover enough of the options. This is why application management seems to be settling in as the accepted term, at least among the consultants and analysts that were surveyed during the research for this book.

Much like infrastructure and VMs, applications have a lifecycle that must be managed. They are purchased, deployed, updated, and maybe even retired at some point. Although we all know that some terrible applications seem to live on forever, it is the reason many organizations do some of these EUC projects. The following are a number of points that should be included as part of the application management for your apps. Some of these are the same for any application management alternative while others may be different for each or some alternatives.

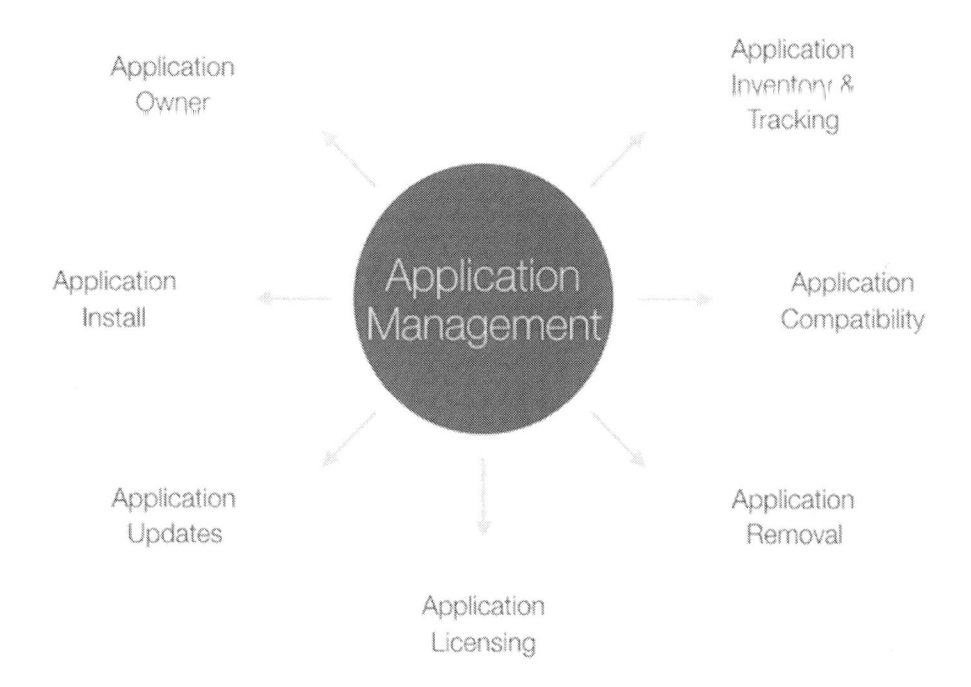

- Application Owner
- Application Inventory & Tracking
- Application Install
- Application Compatibility
- Application Updates
- Application Removal
- Application Licensing

(Application Management)

Application Owner

The application owner is not a feature found in any application management tool, but it is a very important piece of information. There are tons of different applications in the business world today. Some are purchased, while others are written in-house. There are many applications that are purchased that may not have an application owner, but most do. If the application is critical to business or is revenue generating, you can bet that there is a person or department within the organization that is responsible for it.

By working with the application owner you will gain access to detailed history, requirements, and usage of their application. Some owners are better than others, as turnover throughout the years can lead to loss in tribal knowledge. The app owner can help identify people and teams that use and rely on the application when you do not have a detailed inventory of all users. They also can provide install and licensing facts that will be explained in the following sections.

Working with the owner should also help identify what the real access and availability requirements are for their application. This is helpful beyond an end user that says they must use it 24/7/365. You can also work with them to explain and discuss prospective application management and presentation options as part of the design if they are not already being used today.

Application Inventory and Tracking

Having a good application dependency map was discussed in Chapter 5. This is something every organization needs, and few have a good handle on. The idea is simple; you need a list of all the applications installed in the environment. You will also need to know if there are multiple versions, which ones are actively used, and by how many users. It would also be great if you know how they accessed them.

To accomplish this, you are going to need a tool for this job. If you think you can do this with some scripts and PowerShell, then you have too much free time and little grip on reality. You may or may not be able to use the same tool for the assessment and the ongoing tracking. There are a number of tools such as Microsoft SCCM and other PC Lifecycle Management (PCLM) tools that offer this type of feature. They typically have an agent that is installed on all of your endpoints and report back a ton of data that is consumed in pre-built or ad-hoc reports.

You will need to have a solid handle on the application usage and access for inventory, licensing, capacity planning, and lifecycle functions. Just as you would be able to quickly provide the number of virtual desktops running in your environment, management or some auditor is going to want the same and possibly more details about the applications.

These details will be very valuable to have on the new EUC environment as well as your legacy physical PC environment. Keep in mind when evaluating options, unless you are converting 100% of users to your new EUC design, you will have some legacy.

Application Install

Understanding the application install process seems like a stupid simple problem- you just load up the file and click Next, Next, Finish, and everything is ready to rock. The point is even with Microsoft and other well-known business applications, there can be complex install procedures and requirements. The relationship built with the application owner is a good place to look for details around the install process and any challenges.

If your organization does not have an experienced or dedicated application packaging team, it would be an excellent idea to create documentation around the install process for each application entering your EUC environment. The install process may vary based upon the application management method that is selected. You may be able to follow the basic install process when natively installing the application on Windows, but the process could have multiple different steps that need to be accounted for when installing on an application server or in a virtualized container.

If you plan to offer more than one application method, you will need to document the install process for each method. There will also be testing required for each method to ensure that the application works as expected or if it fails that it is documented why and that the particular method is not available for the application.

Application Compatibility

To be discovered and explored as part of the application installation and testing process, is also is determining application compatibility. Within modern EUC designs, like the ones being discussed in this book, there are potentially a number of compatibilities that could be discovered. You will want to know which OS versions the software does and does not work with, and what software dependencies does the install require. For example, this application may install .Net 3.5 and only work with that version. Also, it only works with a specific version of Java or something like this. If you were just installing one application this would not be an issue.

It is likely that you are installing a number applications on desktops and on application servers that will be presented to users. These compatibility constraints can affect how you are able to offer applications to users. Will there be more application servers used to create isolation for applications that do not play nice with others? Can you use some other isolation method to remove some of these incompatibilities? These are all questions that need to be explored and tested for your application landscape.

You cannot afford to create specific desktops just so users can have access to a terrible application that no one is willing to upgrade or retire. This type of approach will cause sprawl in your environment and complicate the management story. The good news is that this does not all have to be manual testing anymore. There are companies that offer tools that help with this problem. In the old days, this was a long and soul-breaking process, but tools from Citrix, Flexera, and others can dramatically reduce the time and effort.

Application Updates

Through the lifecycle of an application there are going to be updates that are required. These updates may be to support new OS, new features, and one of many other reasons. In the business world some applications have very limited updates, while in the consumer world most are used to the constant siege of updates. Anyone that uses a web browser or applications on your mobile device is used to being nagged on a daily or weekly basis to upgrade to get the latest feature or to fix a bug.

As each application is examined before management alternatives are evaluated, knowing how many and how often an application is updated will be useful. Based on the application and use case requirements, one or several alternatives will be selected. You will also need to understand what the level of effort will be for each update. You are concerned as an admin at the office level for the support stuff, but if updates are common, you will want to consider how this will or will not be noticed by the users. Ideally, they would have no idea that an application was updated, unless there was a visible version displayed or new features were easily visible.

Updates will be run through the compatibility phase that was just discussed to ensure the new version will play nicely with others. Just as it was a pain to update an application natively installed on thousands of PCs, it will be just as painful if it is installed that way on thousands of VMs.

Application Removal

While removing an application or access to an application might be not that common of a request, you cannot ignore this process. There are plenty of reasons that might drive a request to remove an application from a user or a group of users. This could be a job change, an application being retired, or just reducing the number of users to save on licensing costs. Depending on which application management alternative chosen, this could be as simple as removing login privileges or could require the application to be uninstalled from a device. This is just another part of the process to make sure that is clear when evaluating the different alternatives and what each one has to offer.

Application Licensing

To most, application licensing is easy- if you install it on 50 PCs you need 50 licenses for the application. There are, however, probably thousands of lawyers in the world that make their living off of working with software vendors over licensing complaints. Software licensing can be a very sticky discussion, especially when using and accessing it in ways that it was never intended on before all of these cool EUC options existed. For example, some software licensing is different whether it is installed on a PC directly or running on a PC or VM in the data center, especially for Microsoft. While others may have different licensing concerns on the number of users at a single point (concurrency) or the number of users that are entitled to access it. These can lead to very different costs when building your design or application method.

In Non-Persistent desktop pools, a user may not get the same desktop every time, applications will need to have some sort of network or volume license option. If the application license is tied to the computer, the pool may need to be a dedicated non-persistent pool.

Although many applications now have some network licensing server, such as FLEXlm or Microsoft KMS, there are still applications that may be licensed to a particular computer or some sort of hardware key. This can be the case with older applications or programs that are licensed through a retail channel. If the application is licensed with a USB hardware key, you may need to utilize a USB-over-IP Hub to use the application in a virtual environment.

Once you understand the licensing for each application, most organizations will want or need a method to understand what licenses are being consumed for each application. This will help audit their usage and exposure to further expenses if not controlled properly. Working with the application owner to determine the licensing model and how they are or could be tracked will be critical. You will then understand if there is a tracking method in place already, or whether you need to identify other options.

Application Management Alternatives

The first part of the chapter covered many of the important attributes that should be considered when looking at application management alternatives. The remainder of the chapter will cover each of the management alternatives, explaining how the technology works and if it helps or does not change any of the attributes discussed earlier.

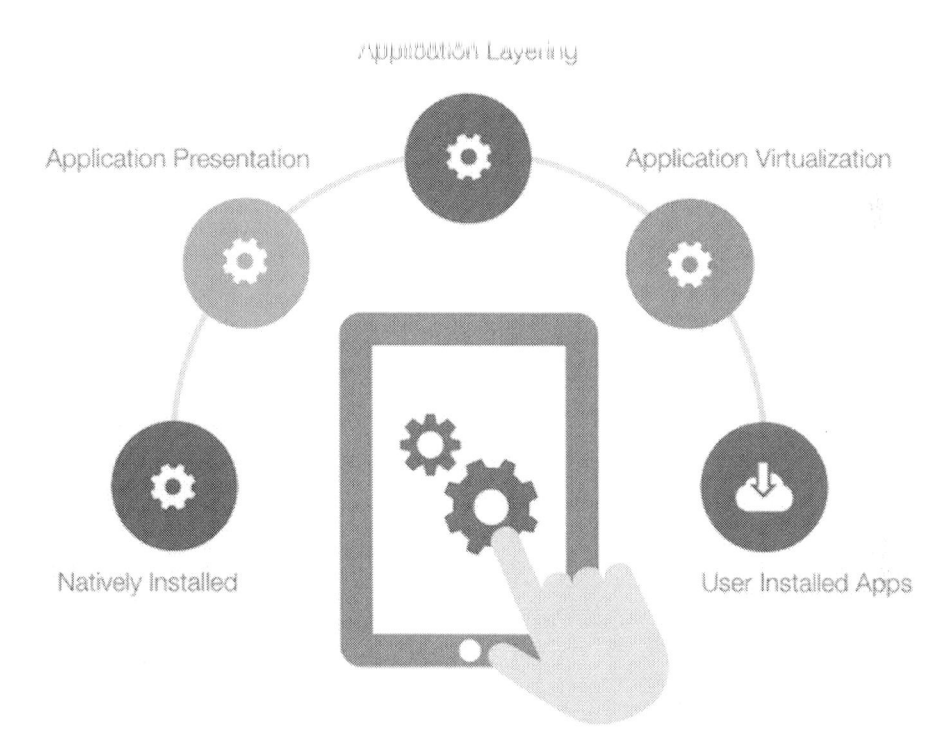

Application Layering

Application Presentation

Application Virtualization

Natively Installed

User Installed Apps

Application Management Alternatives

Natively Installed

When an application is installed directly on the OS, just as the software developer had intended, this is a native install. This is typically and 1:1 relationship between the application and the OS, meaning this has to be repeated for each OS copy that wishes to use the application. When you install an application on your laptop or desktop computer this is natively installed.

98 | *Architecting EUC Solutions*

This is the most common application alternative when dealing with physical computers even in modern times. The process to natively install an application is typically very easy with few constraints. You usually follow the installer prompts, and it will tell you if you are missing any dependencies or just automatically add them for you. When it finishes you are ready to start using the app.

While the process to install apps on your own device yourself is very easy, if you intend on installing the same app on hundreds or thousands of devices, that is a whole different challenge. To accomplish application installs to a large group of machines will require some type of automation or a tool to make the task more manageable. Historically, taking a scripting approach to automating the install of an application may have been the cheaper method, but it is also the more time consuming approach. Creating and then maintaining the script can be very time consuming. If the person that created the script is no longer around, it can become a broken process quickly. You will also need a script for every application that you plan to deploy in this manner, and a way to create a target list of systems to install the app onto. Also, you have to think about if can you create a workflow if you have to deploy 10 apps at once or would they need to be all done in a serial process. This approach leads to early graying of your and your boss's hair.

Another approach to getting applications installed would be to use Windows Group Policy (GPO). Through the use of GPP/GPO you can create policies and apply them to groups that will push the application out. While this offers more structure than a manual scripting process, it does create a large management burden for managing the users/workstations that must be added and removed from these groups. This approach would work in both a physical and virtual desktop environment. This method can lengthen the startup time of a machine to several minutes as the GPO client must evaluate all applied GPOs.

The most popular approach in large environments is to use a tool for this application install and push to users and workstations. For this approach, applications would be packaged into an MSI format and pushed out via groups or policies created within the tool. These tools typically have an agent installed on the endpoint OS that communicates back inventory and system details. This will allow admins to understand what is installed on the endpoint and with system resources. These tools are helpful for the initial install as well as an updates that must be pushed out. The inventory ability can greatly increase your visibility into how successful the application push was. In the previous methods, you would need another method to see if the installs were successful. There are a number of tools that can do this; some of the better known ones are Microsoft SCCM, LANDesk, and Altiris.

The native install options discussed above are used most commonly for deploying applications to laptops, physical PCs and full clone (persistent) virtual desktops (VDI). These are all individual OS instances, and each are their own unique snowflake that has to be managed as such. These snowflakes are relatively easy to get applications installed on since it is what has been done for the past 20+ years. Managing them and updating is the challenging part. If you have these types of targets it will be up to the design team to try and limit where possible the amount of native applications to reduce the support effort. Using some of the following management alternatives can help with this effort.

The other place that people have natively installed applications is into the master, parent or golden image. These images are used in non-persistent VDI provisioning methods such as VMware Linked Clones or Citrix MCS/PVS. These provisioning models allow or a single OS image to be used to provision a large pool of desktops that all start from this read only image. This master image can also have applications installed as part of it. This is commonly referred to as baking them into the image. Since you are really just natively installing the apps into your image, this is a very easy method to get things going quickly.

By baking in applications in your image, you can severally limit the number of use cases that can use a given image. This can lead to an increased number of master images that will need to be used to create additional smaller desktop pools to accommodate the application assignments required. While baking applications in is easy to start, it quickly increases the complexity of the design and adds additional management overhead by increasing the number of pools and images that must be maintained. This is another reason to have a firm understanding of your requirements before starting. You will also need to track the changes for each image, which can be time consuming, to be able to understand what the differences between the different images are.

This is not to say that baking in a few applications is forbidden; you should just look to do this for a minimal subset of apps. The best apps to bake into an image would be ones that are universally used by a majority of your use cases. This might be things like a particular web browser, a PDF reader, and maybe Microsoft Office. If these apps are used by the greater user population and there is not a need to provide multiple versions, than baking them in maybe a suitable option. For applications that are not baked into the image, you can use another application management alternative to provide application access based on use case or user requirements.

When applications are baked into an image you must take a copy of your master image and install the app updates. Then follow the process to insert the newly updated master image into the provisioning tool so that pool can use the updated image. Note that all desktops within the pool that you updated the image for will immediately, or on a schedule, be forced to use the newly updated image. This is important to note that app updates if baked in are going to affect the entire pool(s) of desktops that are using a given image.

Application Presentation

Outside of the natively installed applications, application presentation is the most mature of the application management alternatives. With Terminal Services and early Citrix versions having roots back 20 years, there is a deep history and deployments in this space. The idea and concept has not changed greatly through the years- you host applications on servers in the data center that present the application out to endpoints. This is done with a client, and it is

Architecting EUC Solutions | 101

essentially just showing screen scrapes to the endpoint while sending back input requests.

This alternative makes it possible to host and present nearly any Windows based application to pretty much any endpoint available in the market today. Vendors support presenting the apps via an HTML5 session in a browser or a client that is offered on nearly every platform today. To accomplish this, servers are grouped into silos or farms that host and present a common set of applications. To deal with compatibility, scale, and segmentation requirements a number of different silos or farms are created based on needs and scale.

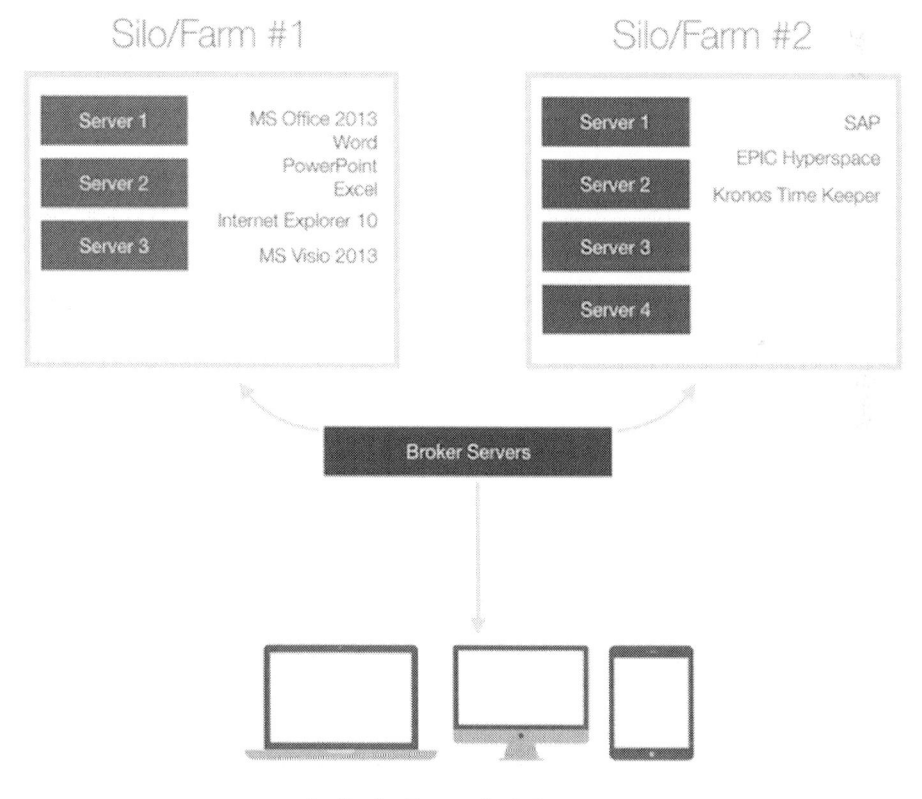

Silo/Farm #1

Server 1	MS Office 2013
Server 2	Word
	PowerPoint
	Excel
Server 3	Internet Explorer 10
	MS Visio 2013

Silo/Farm #2

Server 1	SAP
Server 2	EPIC Hyperspace
	Kronos Time Keeper
Server 3	
Server 4	

Broker Servers

Application Presentation Infrastructure

The core for this technology is Microsoft Remote Desktop Session Hosts (RDSH), which translate to Terminal Services if you have been doing IT for a long time. Third-party vendors build their products on top of RDSH to extend the capabilities and offer more robust offerings. Since it is based on Microsoft OS, you are limited to presenting Windows-based applications or ones that can be consume via a web browser.

By using this alternative, applications are installed centrally on a limited number of servers. This reduces application management by only having a limited number of servers to update when the application is patched or updated to a new version. As a result of the updates the clients consuming the app has access to the newly updated application. This is a large time reduction when apps are consumed by large numbers of users, especially for apps that are updated often.

Another benefit of hosting apps centrally is that compatibility and OS constraints can be removed from endpoints. If there is a legacy app that does not work on 64 bit OS or only works on an OS that you no longer use, you can account for this in the server farm and present out to your endpoints without constraining them to the apps limitations. This also works when use cases need access to multiple version of the same application. The users could be consuming Access 2013 as part of their normal build, while and older version of Access is presented to them from a server farm.

The infrastructure required for these solutions are typically Windows server VMs. You can, of course, still use physical Windows servers, but who does that anymore? The size and number of the Windows servers will vary greatly depending on number of applications, farms and users that are going to be accessing. Typically, you are going to see average user density in the 20-50 user range per RDSH server. There will be cases where less or more users are possible of course.

With different farms, applications and multiple servers the vendor needs to provide a way of easily assigning applications and load balancing requests across the servers. Each of the major vendors offers this ability, but there is a gap between how well each of them do it, and with what options they provide.

This is something to understand better as you work through your design for accessibility and resilience between sites if required.

As far as limitations or drawbacks in this alternative, there are very few with the technology being very mature. You may still find a few 16 bit apps and you will be bound to an older 32 bit OS. You may also still find a couple of applications that do not behave well in a multi-user server install. Of these many the bugs can be worked out with just a minimal amount that will not work at all.

The major risks in designing and deploying application presentation in your organization would be improper sizing of servers for user density and underestimating the amount of time and effort to install applications. The effort to install and test applications in this and other alternatives can be time consuming. If you are new to this approach, and have a large number of applications, be sure to understand just how long you will need to account for in your project plan.

Application Layering

Application layering is one of the newer application management alternatives with the majority of the products being one to two years old in the market. Some of the leading products in the layering space are VMware App Volumes, Citrix AppDisks, Liquidware Labs FlexApp, and Unidesk.

This means that it is still an alternative that is maturing and has some constraints that are still being worked out of the different products. The idea is simple- you have your OS that is on your physical device or a VM, and a virtual disk is attached to the OS and through an agent the application is layered on top of the OS.

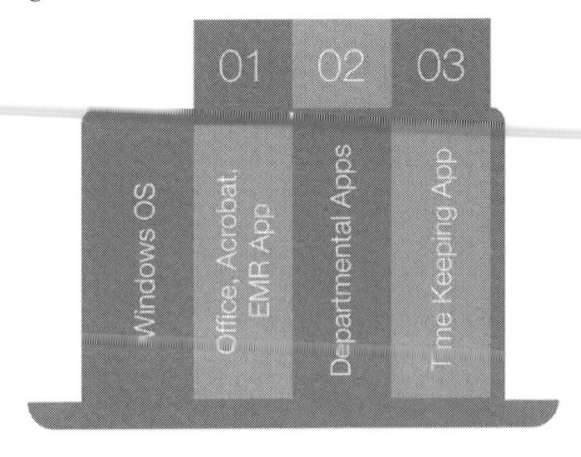

Application Layering

The app layers are captured or bundled into these virtual disks, and each layer can contain a single or multiple applications. Typically, most products cannot natively restrict visibility to certain applications if the layer has multiple apps in it. This means that if you create a layer with 10 applications, whoever that layer is assigned to will be able to use all 10 applications. This may or may not be of concern to you, but it could have licensing implications as mentioned earlier in the chapter.

The idea of application layering is great, and is something that the non-persistent VDI market has needed for years. You can now have a single master image, and through application layering be able to present applications to users based upon their user IDs, machines, or some Active Directory structure. This flexibility helps reduce the number of master images by not needing to natively install applications into them, as mentioned earlier. The layers can also be updated as applications are updated, and then presented to only those users that are consuming the newly updated layer. This approach is a streamlined workflow for admins to follow and reduces the number of users that are touched.

Architecting EUC Solutions | 105

For most products there is a pretty simple process to creating an app layer. This is typically done by creating a VM that will be used as the OS for the apps to be installed on. A new virtual disk is mounted to the capture machine as a blank app layer, and any application changes such as a newly installed application are captured in this layer. The virtual disk is then removed from the capture VM, checked into the management layer, and then made available to users. How you install the applications into a new layer is up to the admin. You can typically use existing methods if already available. If you have already packaged applications and have them in SCCM to push to physical devices, you can likely use the same process to push the app into your new layer.

Depending on the vendor's product, you typically have the option of assigning the layer to the OS at the time of boot up or when the user logs into the OS. If the layer is applied at boot, you are really assigning the application layer to the device and if it is applied at user login you assigning it to the user. By assigning layers to the user you have the flexibility of allowing the user to log into any Windows device that has the layering agent, and their applications will be there for them to use. By assigning to the device at boot you are assigning the applications to a pool of desktops, which is less flexible in some designs.

There are some limits to application layering, first of which is the number of layers that can be mounted to a single target. This is usually a limiting factor of Windows at this time. While evaluating layering alternatives, this is a point to research. You do not or should not have the need to attach dozens of layers to a single VM each with a single application in them. If you use a sensible layering strategy, being constrained to 10-20 layers per VM should not be an issue.

Application layering does not do any type of application isolation like app virtualization offers. This is discussed later in this chapter.

To accommodate any potential layer limits, a strategy of creating application layers based on enterprise apps, department apps, and then app-specific layers. The enterprise app layers would contain apps that are broadly assigned to every user or the majority of users in the organization. A departmental app stack would be all of the applications commonly assigned to accounting specific use case. There would be a layer created for each department that has a use case assigned to it. Then there would be individual app layers created for applications that did not fall into these other categories. There may be other opportunities to bundle apps together into layers also. This would leave most uses cases with 10 or less app layers applied to them, keeping you clear of most limits.

Some other constraints that exist for most application layering offering today are around how they are backed up and replicated for disaster recovery. Since each layer is a virtual disk file of some format and not always attached to a VM, or the same VM. This typically makes them next to impossible to backup with your existing backup products. For the same reason, it makes them just as challenging to replication them to another site for disaster recovery. Application layering is quickly becoming a popular alternative in most modern EUC designs. Check on these limits when evaluating to see if they still existing. This will allow you to accommodate any constraints in your design.

What type of infrastructure is required to provide application layering? For most solutions the infrastructure is minimal. There are typically one to several management servers. These servers are typically VMs that would run in your management cluster. They are used to manage the layers and broker the connections to layering targets. The layers will be stored on a shared datastore for the hypervisor and layering product to access. Once a product is selected, consult their reference architectures to understand what they require for minimal performance. Be sure to also check some recommend multiple copies of each app layer to spread the load across multiple virtual disks.

Finally, it is important for you to understand how performance is affected with apps being layered on. The good news is that they usually perform just like natively installed apps on your OS. The only thing to consider about performance and app layering is this method does increase the amount of CPU consumed by a VM that is using app layers. The answer to that question is if you are applying the layers at the time of user login, then yet. There is currently

Architecting EUC Solutions | 107

a 20-30% brief increase in CPU usage of the VM at logon while the apps are layered in. This CPU usage bump is typically 5-10 seconds depending on the environment, but is something to keep in mind when sizing your hosts.

Applications Virtualization

Application virtualization is capturing an application that will run in an encapsulated environment when executed. This is also referred to as application streaming, sandboxed apps, and a few other terms. There are a number of different products in the market that provide this ability, several of them have been acquired by the large EUC vendors, and rolled into their suite based product offerings.

Once an application has been captured and prepared in the virtualization product, it is available as a single file or a small number of files. These typically appear as .exe, .msi or .appv file extensions, depending on the product used to capture the application. The application package that runs in a bubble or sandbox, allows the application to run isolated from other apps running on the same OS. Within the package all of the files that are installed or changed during the application install process are captured as part of the package. This includes all .DLL files, .ini files, registry updates and any other changes.

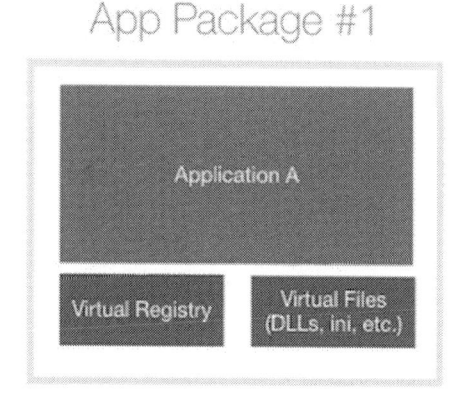

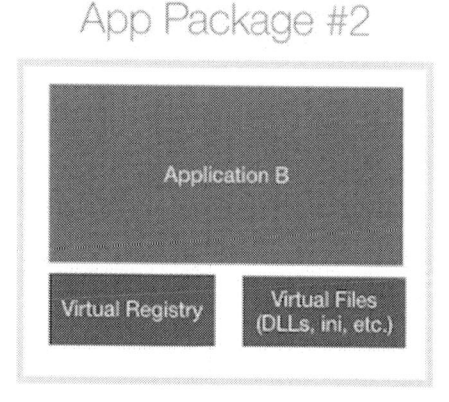

App Package #1

Application A

Virtual Registry | Virtual Files (DLLs, ini, etc.)

App Package #2

Application B

Virtual Registry | Virtual Files (DLLs, ini, etc.)

One of the best benefits of running an application in an isolated bubble like this is the ability to run two different versions of the same application without any conflicts. This can be helpful when you have a use case that needs to run two different versions of MS Access, as an example. You can also control how the isolated app can interact with the OS, file system, and other applications on the same host. This allows you to range from fully isolating the app to making it more feel like its natively running.

While there are a few nice benefits from virtualized apps, there are also a number of challenges and constraints. This starts with the capturing process to packing applications. In this alternative, this is probably the most challenging aspect and has a lower success rate than other options. Getting apps to run in these isolated bubbles takes more time and tweaking to get them to operate normally. There are also some apps that are just not compatible immediately because of dependencies that they have. This will vary based on the product that you select.

You have the option of capturing a single application in a package or capturing multiple applications in a single package. This can be done to allow the needed dependencies to exist in the same package, versus trying to ensure a dependency is always available in the host OS. To allow virtualized applications to work with other packages, you can create links between packages to allow them to communicate and function more like natively installed applications. These are explicit and must be done at packaging time or updated later, as they are not automatic.

The packages are typically stored in a central repository and streamed to endpoints when users open the application. Depending on how the applications cache data on endpoints and the performance of your network, there can be a difference in application performance versus installed apps, layered apps, or presented apps. There is also the possibility of pushing the packages out to each endpoint for better performance. This creates additional management overhead and creates the challenge of keeping the remote packages updated when applications are patched. These virtualized apps can only be run by Windows OS clients and cannot be presented and used on mobile, Linux, or Mac clients.

Infrastructure required for capturing and presenting virtualized applications varies widely between vendors. From the minimal side all that is required is a VM on which to capture application and a network accessible file share, while other vendors require a heavier management experience that also includes backend management servers.

There are a small subset of app virtualizers that think it is the greatest method, and use it for every application that is compatible. While the majority view, this alternative as a nice option to have in your tool belt. Remember, though, it should only be used when the requirements clearly call for the isolation that is provided, as there are other methods to provide multiple versions of the same app to use cases.

User Installed Applications

Letting users install applications has been happening since computers were first invented and used in organizations. In fact, this was about the only way apps were usable in the early days. As large organizations adopted computers at scale, letting end users install whatever they wanted lead to problems. Most environments where computers were not locked down and controlled by policy, are plagued by higher than normal support efforts for desktops.

In the early days of VDI, organizations almost always went the persistent VDI route. This allowed them to treat the virtual desktops just like physical desktops, and kept the same practices. Their ultimate goal usually was to create a more locked down and secure environment for desktops, while still providing users the tools they need to perform their work. This was met with resistance or lack of time and usually got forgotten about.

With persistent virtual desktops, allowing user installable apps is as easy as giving them the permission to install applications. Since they each have their own virtual desktop, and all of their data and apps are contained within that one snowflake desktop, there is little challenge around this request outside of permissions. Most organizations had the desire to adopt non-persistent desktops to take advantage of the operational savings of using the single master image. If forced to allow user installed apps, they were forced back to persistent desktops or not provide desktops to that use case. Over the past couple of years, new solutions that offered the ability to have a user writable disk attach to non-persistent VMs has become available. This would allow any changes to be captured during a non-persistent session, and have them persistent for the user permanently- sounds like magic and the problem is solved.

Well, not exactly. Today these user writable volumes are now part of most application layering products that were discussed earlier. While the technology has made it possible to allow this, you will still be plagued by higher support effort if there is not good policy set around these requests. It may be better to have a whitelist of what is allowed versus allowing anything to be installed.

These user writable volumes add complexity to the design and are constrained by some of the same limitations that the application layering volumes have. Today you may lose VM mobility when a writable volume is attached to it. The volumes are still very difficult to take backups of and replicate to another site for disaster recovery protection. These constraints pose a large risk to the design. If there is a real business case to allow this feature, then there is a real business need to be able to recover these volumes in the event of a disaster.

Since these are part of most application layering products they use the same management infrastructure that the layering features use. They will require shared storage of decent performance for the writable volumes to be stored on. This means that they cannot go on slow disk like user files, but also do not require an all flash solution.

Summary

As mentioned multiple times throughout the book and this chapter that applications are and should be a focal point in your design and project. The good thing is that there are a number of great alternatives on how to manage and present applications to use cases today. The drawback is most of them have a licensing cost attached to them as does any good piece of software.

Let the requirements from your use cases lead you in the evaluation of application management alternatives. Do not be afraid of mixing products from different vendors if that provides the best solution. While the product offerings from Citrix and VMware have gotten very mature, sometime the best design uses a blended approach.

[10]
User Profiles

A user profile is a collection of all the unique settings for an individual user. They are also referred to as user persona or user environment management (UEM). There are several terms for this. While definition of each of them is different, the goal is to present the same user experience to the end user on any desktop that they log into. User environment management expands past just profiles to include policies and additional settings.

Why should you be concerned about capturing and managing user profiles? The short answer is that you need to be able to ensure a consistent user experience across the different services within your EUC design. In the early days of VDI it was much like the beginning of server virtualization, admins did the same things in the virtual environment as they did with their physical servers. With desktops, this means exclusively using persistent fully cloned desktop VMs from a template or a legacy deployment tool, that would install the OS and applications just like on a physical desktop.

While this approach worked then and still can work today, it provided little operational value and only really allowed users to remotely connect to their work desktop from any location. In a sense, the burden was just moved from a device to a VM and in many cases there was still a physical device to deal with as well. With a persistent virtual desktop each one is unique like a snowflake, which means they must all be patched and updated individually for OS and application patches. If you have any number of these that was a large effort, it also meant so the users profile was part of the persistent VM, just as it would have been part of the physical PC in the past.

If a profile management tool was not being used, the users profile would only be available in that single persistent desktop. Over the years the tools and application delivery options have improved significantly, and the goal of non-persistent desktops is a reality. This means that the desktop VM that a user logs into is completely disposable and is refreshed on a regular basis. This is accomplished by capturing the users profile and layering it on at the time of login. This way the user gets their consistent experience and updates are captured, but they can log into any desktop or VM that has the profile management solution enabled.

Another place that managed profiles have been used for a long time is in application presentation or remoting solutions such as Citrix XenApp or other Microsoft RDS based options. These allow the application to be presented to any device for the user to work with. In this case, the user still has application related settings such as the personal dictionary in MS Word or an email signature that needs to be captured so the user does not feel like they are working on the community PC in a hotel lobby.

Profile Management Options

There are a number of different vendors and tools available in the market today for managing a user's profile. Some of them are free; some are provided in suite based licensing from the brokering vendor; and most are third-party vendors that charge for user based licensing. In a short survey of what products the author team has seen in their customer experience, as well as talking with other EUC experts, there appears to be 15-20 profile tools available today. The reality is that we have only seen a handful of these deployed in the field. The following is a summary of the most recognizable profile tools. The list does not rank them in any order and is not meant to imply that tools not on the list are not worth evaluating.

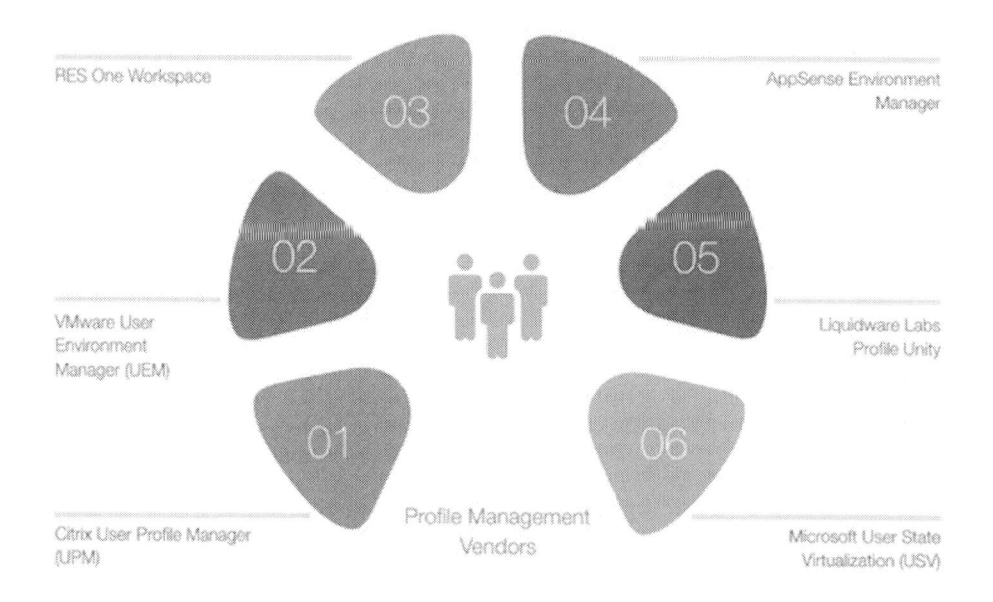

RES One Workspace — 03
AppSense Environment Manager — 04
VMware User Environment Manager (UEM) — 02
Liquidware Labs Profile Unity — 05
Citrix User Profile Manager (UPM) — 01
Microsoft User State Virtualization (USV) — 06

Profile Management Vendors

Citrix UPM - UPM was an acquisition for Citrix a long time ago. The product has changed little over the years but has seen a lot of deployment in XenApp and XenDesktop environments. The tool is relatively simple and gets the job done for a number of customers.

VMware UEM - User Environment Manager is the Immidio product that VMware acquired in early 2015. UEM is solution that VMware and partners are now leading with for deployments when considering the Horizon Suite. VMware still offers View Persona Manager that was acquired several years ago and has seem mixed results in the field. The former Immidio product was already a mature offering and had recorded some very large deployments in Europe.

RES One Workspace - Workspace has long been the main AppSense competitor, being one of the first products to be able to match the advanced features. RES has a loyal following of customers and consultants that speak highly of the product. Along with profiles and user environment, RES also has an impressive automation tool and service store that are both focused on providing a modern self-service EUC experience.

AppSense Environment Manager - This is the heavy weight in the profile space and has been for several years. AppSense has long had the reputation of being the most feature rich, but also the most expensive by a fair margin. For several years EM was able to do things that others could not, many of those gaps have been closed by some of the main vendors. They were the first tool that allowed you to remove a lot of actions and controls from group policy and apply them at the profile layer, this helped improve login times for many.

Liquidware Labs Profile Unity - The LWL teams has been around the profile game for a long time now, and has worked closely with both Citrix and VMware to help customers. The profile unity tool has matured a long way in the past two years, and is now a worthy competitor to anyone. The solution is pretty simple and quick to deploy and start managing users' profiles. Liquidware also produces some great assessment and monitoring tools for EUC projects.

MS user state virtualization - USV from Microsoft is more of a slight of hand trick than a new product. Back around 2010 they saw the light that these third-party vendors were turning out some good products and there was a real need for profile management, so they renamed stuff they've had laying around. The USV solution is basically the updated version of roaming profiles, folder redirection and offline files that have been around for a long time without any fancy name attached to it. With all that said there have been small improvements over the years, but they are still roaming profiles. There are still a significant amount of customers that have deployed this because they were familiar with the technology and it's free, hard to argue with free sometimes.

Features to consider

The most important feature is likely flexibility. You want the tool to be easy to use and setup. That way, if the tool captures all user settings for you, by default it will allow you to begin testing and tuning sooner. If needed, you can use granular tweaks to exclude settings, folders, or files that are not needed or are

Architecting EUC Solutions | 117

bloating the size of profiles. There is a fine line to walk on flexibility, the tools range from capture everything thing with a few tweaks to having a massive amount of individual settings. You want the flexibility, but not be overwhelmed.

The ability to offer context aware as a feature has long been reserved to the most expensive of profile tools. Now it is becoming a mainstream feature. Context awareness allows for some type of variable to be monitored and have actions are taken upon what was discovered. An example of this might be to watch to see from where the user is connecting. If they are internal on the corporate network, the design will let them perform more actions. If, however, they are remotely connecting, a few applications may be restricted from them. The ability to offer this is very helpful, but is not needed for all deployments.

The ability to trigger an action based on something is another feature that can be helpful to several scenarios. An example of this would be if a user opens an application it will automatically add a printer that is only used for that application. When the app is closed the printer is removed, this is done with no interaction by the user. One idea around this is it can keep a number of settings from having to be applied at login and are only done when needed.

The days of giving all of your users local admin rights to their desktops is gone; and if it is not, then it should be. Having admin rights only leads to heartbreaks from the operations team. Taking away these elevated rights does present some challenges that admins have learned to deal with in different ways. Some of the profile tools have the ability to elevate user or application rights when the request meets policies set. Let's talk through a couple of simple examples. You may have an application that cannot run unless it has admin rights and your users do not have that, so the ability to allow just the application to run with elevated rights is helpful. A second example would be to create policies around a few applications that you do approve of users to install and you configure elevated rights for those installers. This will allow the users to install the approved application without issues when they are ready if needed.

This is much less of a problem these days. In the past, though, there could be challenges of users moving back and further between desktops that used different Microsoft profile versions. For example, with organizations heavily invested in Windows 7, there will be eventually a moved towards Windows 8 or more likely Windows 10. During those times, you will need to ensure how the tools you evaluate will deal with migrations if needed, and if users can work in both versions.

Things to Watch Out For

There were a few things to watch out for in the previous section that covered a popular set of features to look at during your evaluation. In this section the focus is more on things that can affect your performance negatively. You will want to closely look at how the solutions capture, package, and synchronize the user settings. You are looking for something that is efficient and lightweight. If you remember, the main pain point with the original roaming profiles was once the profile grew the log on and log out times were extended while the profile was copied down or back up. This was so you go the most recent version that synced changes when leaving, but the method was very inefficient, and slowed things down badly.

Today most tools are advanced enough that they only need to copy or synchronize the portions of the profile that have changed, greatly reducing the amount of data that is moved. Along with this idea, identify how and where the profiles will be stored, and what affects that could have if there was an outage. For example, are the profiles simply stored on a file share in the data center or are they stored in a central database? With either of these options, you will want to learn how they are made highly available and how you would diagnose if there was a performance issue with profiles to understand if the backend repository was part of the issue.

Risks of Folder Redirection

While using just folder redirection is not the way to architect your profile management solution, it is part of nearly every alternative that includes one of the vendor or third-party tools. For this reason, you must understand the risks associated with folder redirection and how you would deal with them.

The most obvious problem would be what if the redirection fails because the file share is down, a DNS problem, a GPO change or one of many other reasons. In this scenario you can expect that users will not have access to their documents and other folders that were redirected, it can also affect applications that rely on the redirected content. This will lead to a surge of user complaints and tickets, because users will be looking for missing files or unable to use a needed application. Elevating your monitoring of these file services and servers is a highly recommended step in ensuring you are reacting quickly or fixing before things are noticed by users.

How can the performance of a file server affect the user experience? Dramatically. If you are using Windows file servers and the CPU usage reaches well into the 90 percent range the performance is going to drop off the cliff. This is going to negatively affect anything that is using folder redirection to that file server. Users are going to experience serious delays in browsing, opening, and saving files. If parts of the profile are redirected there or the profile tool is using this file server there are a number of Windows functions that can be negatively affected. Things as simple as how the start menu performs or a search for a program can take 30 seconds to several minutes, rather than the five seconds or less that is normal.

This is what makes sizing your file servers or NAS appliance for your workloads very critical in these designs. Also, continually monitoring the usable resource to adjust and provide additional resources when needed or determine what might be causing an abnormal spike in resource usage. What might seem like a few seconds of delay on the server side can easily translate to a 5-10x or more delay on the end user side.

Disaster Recovery

The whole disaster recovery discussion is covered in greater detail in Chapter 13, but for the purpose of user profiles there are different things to consider. If you deploy an EUC based solution, whether it is virtual desktops or application presentation, you are almost certainly going to be expected to be able to recover these services in the event of a significant outage. The next question is do you know what your requirements around the recovery will be?

Will you simply be able to present the user with a generic desktop as long as they can access their applications? Will your users tolerate a change in user experience during this time of recovery? If yes, then your job got a lot easier. Typically you will not be so lucky. Your users are going to expect the same user experience and should not notice any difference in their sessions than before the disaster event. For this to take place you will need to protect their user profiles and data.

How you protect the user profiles and data is going to vary based on the vendor and the method they store your data in. It was briefly touched on earlier in the chapter on the different methods that profile vendors use for the backend of their solutions. It is largely either a file share or a database as the backend repository for these. Each of these options has its pros and cons and are very different in how they would be protected and recovered.

Let's start with the file share based solutions since this is the easier to grasp. Many vendors simply require a file share to store the profile bits on. They can vary greatly in how they store them. For the file share, there are a number of solutions that can be used for this that range from a simple Windows server with a shared folder, to a Windows DFSR solution and all the way up to a dedicated NAS appliance. These options range from easy to complex, but also range from single point of failure (SPOF) to highly available. It has been discussed at many points in this design focused book about avoiding SPOF

Architecting EUC Solutions | 121

whenever possible. This is an area that is also very important and can greatly affect the availability and performance of the solution.

The file share can be backed up and restored to the recovery site, it can be replicated to the other site, and it can sit in passive mode until ready or it can be active in both sites. The choice is yours to make and should be based on the requirements from the use cases and the business. Just understand that if you want to be active in both sites it does cut down the options, but also makes for a better highly available solution. Besides just getting the file share recovered in the recovery site there may be some management infrastructure for the profile solution understand how that would be recovered and if it is unavailable to start will that affect users getting their profiles?

On the other side of options are vendors that use a database as the backend repository for the user profiles. These tools can be more complex to plan for disaster recovery if the vendor does not have a good architecture to follow or does not have verified support statements on the different options. Again, like the file share the options can range from a single database server to complex clustered and replicated options. Let the requirements drive your choices here. In this area you are concerned both about having high availability locally within a site, and how it would be recovered to the recovery site.

You will need to research and find out which database solutions the vendor supports, such as Microsoft SQL, Oracle, MySQL, or other options. Then which database highly available options and replication configurations will they support for their product. Examples of this would be do they support SQL failover cluster, AlwaysOn cluster, SQL Mirroring, Oracle RAC are a few. These different database configurations can affect the availability of the database and what options you have for recovery it on the other side and how fast or easy the process will be.

Summary

The user profile layer of the solution is very visible and personal to your users and can make for an excellent or terrible experience. For these reasons you want to spend enough time on this part of your design to ensure that you are successful. It is also something that you must understand how it can negatively affect the user experience and be able to mitigate and be recovered in a disaster.

[11]

Portal

A portal for EUC related services is something that is very hit or miss with customers today. There are organizations that having a portal is a must, others say absolutely not, while a few are open to seeing how it might affect the experience. Historically, the portal in an EUC based deployment was a web page that users could access to see and launch the applications that have be presented to them. These applications were generally presented from servers that were RDS/Terminal server based and would provide a clean method of allowing users to access the applications.

The EUC portal moving forward is becoming far more than just an application launching point. In modern EUC designs the portal is becoming the central point of entitlement and access for all services. To support these needs EUC vendors are maturing old products or have released new ones to provide these additional features.

Entitlement

In the past and even presently, there can be several places to go to entitle users to the EUC services that they need. This can require an admin to access the element managers for several different services with in the EUC design just to entitle a user. This is not something that organizations wish to keep doing, especially as they are looking to adopt EUC services at much larger scale in the future.

The ideal options would be one of the following options: A single point of access for all EUC services or global entitlement of EUC services. By having something like the portal being the single point of access to EUC services, it would be easy for organizations to turn off these services in the event of employee termination. This does not mean that it would make the entitlement easier. It would, however, help with the separation process, which is also a benefit of improved entitlement. When organizations terminate an employee, there is generally a process that must be followed. It is stricter in certain regulated industries. This process must be happening timely and not miss any systems- missing a single service could still allow the ex-employee to access documents if that entitlement was not halted. This makes the need to simplify the entitlement and de-entitlement equally important to many, and even with the turning off of services some times more important.

The second idea of global entitlement would have a single place that would allow admins to entitle users to services. This would likely be the centralized portal. During the process of setting up a new user, the admin would also be enabling access to the required EUC services. Think of this as sort of checking boxes on a list or some other workflow, the end result is that you have granted the user access to the portal and also access to their applications and a virtual desktop from one location. This would shorten the entitlement process for organizations and also cut down on human errors. By having this global entitlement, the de-entitlement process would also be possible by using the same method to remove access to the entitled services.

Single Sign On

The topic of SSO is further covered in the Chapter 17 on security. When discussing SSO with organizations, the point at which users are asked to provide credentials is always a question. Do they log into one of the EUC services and then are not challenged at any other services during that day? Bringing together the SSO method and the EUC portal can be an obvious integration point for most organizations. If the intent is to have users access the services through the portal, then the portal should also be the authentication point. This means that if a third-party SSO product is utilized, the portal must support it. Today most of the EUC vendors that are offering this type of portal are also offering the ability to utilize built in SSO features or different levels of cooperation with third-party SSO vendors.

The intent is to provide a single point of access for services that could also be the single point of authentication. This would allow the user to log into the portal and be challenged for a second factor if needed. The users would then be seamlessly authenticated to any other EUC service and application if supported. An approach like this cuts down on logins required from the end user, and simplifies/ shortens their workflows. It also allows for better control around login security by having this centralized point of authentication that can be used to enforce login policies.

Enterprise App Store

Organizations are very interested in some type of enterprise app store, and the demand will only continue to increase. There has been demand for these features in the past, but the current demand is exploding. This is caused by end users being accustomed to going to the mobile app store on their devices and tapping to get new apps or app updates. This self-service and instant delivery experience is looking to become the standard for enterprise apps in the future.

Historically, application requests were handled by some out of band method, such as inputting a ticket into a support system, waiting for someone to approve it, and then entitling the user to the application or install it for them. This process can take to days and is quickly becoming unacceptable to end users. What organizations are looking to do is create an app store that all or part of their application catalog can be published in. End users can then access the app catalog, and request access to the applications. A natural place for this app store catalog would be in the EUC portal, as the portal becomes the single place to request, access, and authenticate for all services and applications for end users.

To be truly useful, the app store must offer the ability to control access and visibility to applications with policies. Many organizations will not be able to simply load up the application catalog and grant access to their entire user base to consume whatever they want. Through policies, organizations can control who can see which applications, and which ones can be requested with and without authorization. Some applications may be visible to a user, but require a manager's approval before the provisioning is completed. This is a common workflow, as there may be licensing costs or other restrictions, that need to be accounted for.

Architecting EUC Solutions | 127

Approval Workflow

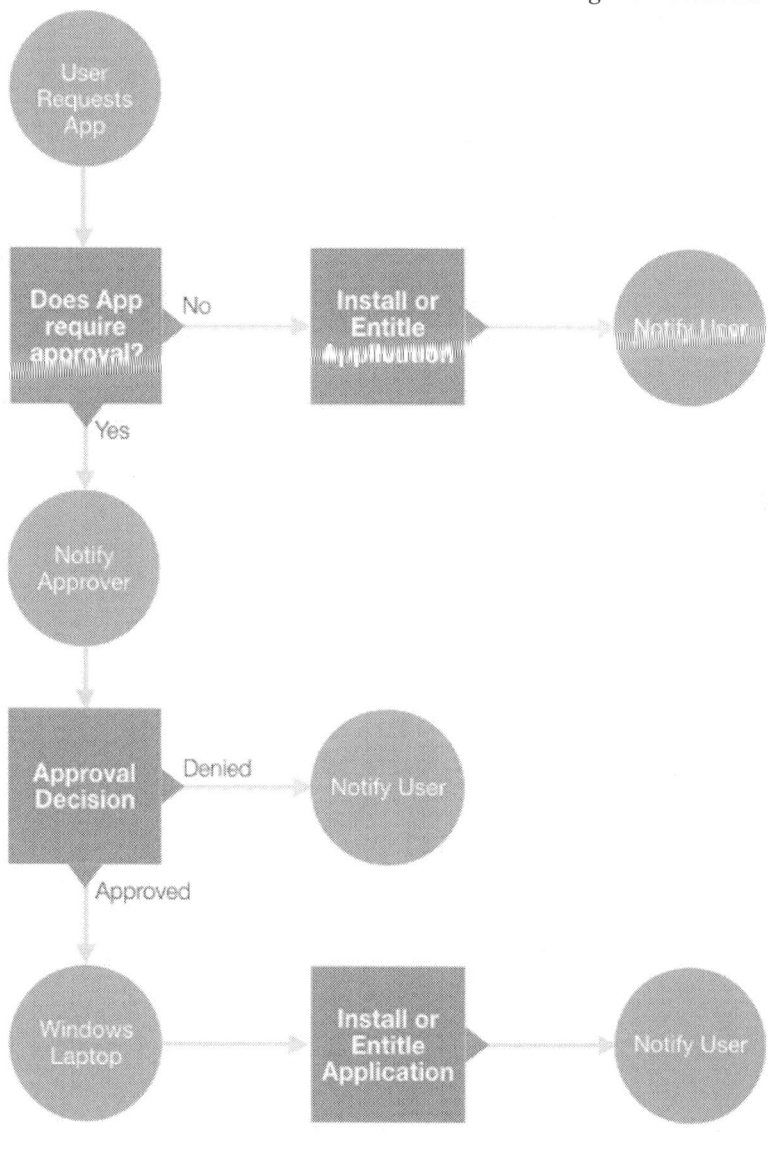

Today some of these features are available in different maturity levels from the vendors. There is still some ways to go for these features to reach what organizations are demanding. As part of the design, it will be important to determine what is the minimal set of requirements that would make these features available today, versus different points in the future as part of your roadmap when some of the other features are expected to be available.

Customization

With all of the features already discussed as part of portal demands, the look and feel of the portal can no longer be generic and rigid. What this means is that minimum table stakes for the portal is to be able to easily brand your organization's portal with logos and company colors. This is typically not too difficult of a task with today's products. The ability to change the look of a portal and add custom content is where things become difficult for most products and organizations today.

With the portal becoming the central point of access and consumption within your design the desire for organizations to publish news, updates and company data on a portal is a very common demand. Some examples would be providing help or links to training documents for consuming EUC services. Ability to publish upcoming maintenance and service disruption notices is a very big demand also. Today's portal products that are included with the EUC product suites are lacking in these advanced customization features. While it might be possible to do some of these modifications, these custom changes are usually unsupported and can be lost during future product upgrades. Being unsupported and upgrade issues add extra risk for organizations that are often too much to overcome.

Summary

Based on the brief discussion in this chapter on EUC portals, it should be clear that portals have been around since the first time Citrix released the web interface, and are maturing to more complicated and feature rich products. It will be important to identify a list of current and future requirements and closely examine what is available today. Organizations might be able to live with what is currently available as the features mature, while others may be required to deploy multiple products to meet their requirements. It is also likely that a simple portal is your best option, and just take a pass on these advanced features, since they are not available and may not be in the near future.

[12]
Disaster Recovery

The topic of disaster recovery (DR) is one that is handled in a wide variety of methods by organizations. Some do nothing, while many have some sort of plan but they vary greatly in scope and effort. A few organizations are extremely prepared for such an event.

The question as it pertains to the topic of this book, is if there is a significant event or disaster to your data center services, will your end users need to work? By moving towards these modern EUC services you are largely centralizing the access points that the end users leverage to do their daily tasks. If there is a significant outage do you need to be able to recover services quickly so they can continue to work?

Your answer is probably yes, or should be yes. Maybe it is not in some organizations. If you do not have a properly defined and tested DR plan for your applications and core data center services, then EUC might not be as important to recover. An example would be if you cannot recover your main revenue generating applications, then the majority of your end users cannot be productive. In this case, giving them their EUC services back before the application may or may not be helpful.

The risk seems too great to not plan and design for DR capabilities from the start. If an organization is serious about EUC, then they will have end users relying on the services. It is likely that the DR solution needs to be marketed properly to get funding.

Vendor Architectures

The remainder of this chapter is going to be covering the different options for DR in the EUC space, along with a list of topics for organizations to consider. As covered earlier, when making your vendor selection the DR options should have been part of the evaluation.

Each of the major vendors provides DR architectures. But all of the vendors, however, go about them in different ways. It is up to the architecture team to understand the different approaches and use this in your evaluation or in the design you create. The following are some details to consider when researching the DR capability of EUC vendors:

- How are they able to handle multiple data centers?
- Number of environments or management interfaces.
- Any manual operations required from staff to fail over?
- How are configurations and entitlements kept in-sync?
- Understand network requirements.

It is up to each organization to determine if any of these items are a negative, positive, or not a factor. The way a vendor deals with a certain architecture may be a turn off for one organization, but may be attractive to another. Figure out what you do not know. Ask questions to learn how the architecture would look and behave in a DR event. Make your decision based upon the facts.

DR Capacity

So your organization is seriously looking at building DR capacity for an EUC project. A question that will come up is how much capacity will the organization need. The next section will cover a few different major architecture alternatives, but the capacity within each alternative can have multiple options.

The capacity discussion should really focus on which services will need to be recovered and the number of users within each of those services. This will lead you down the capacity sizing exercise to meet the DR requirements. The range of requirements can range from 100% of services and users to some percentage of the environment.

Each organization should discover the DR requirements for each use case during the strategy or design phase when they define the requirements for each use case.

Disaster Recovery Alternatives

There are a number of different architecture alternatives. This chapter is going to cover three primary alternatives and look at some of the benefits and challenges of each. The goal is to inspire your thought process and give you guidance when you are rationalizing architecture alternatives. This is an important process for architects. Being able to explain why or why not a decision was made is a key skill.

These are likely not the only three options for providing data center high availability and failover, but they are three common ones. Provided is brief explanation of the different site definitions before taking a deeper look at each alternative.

Active/Active

Both sites actively service user sessions and protect each other.

Active/Warm

Production user sessions from a single site. Warm site for faster recovery.

Active/Cold

All user sessions from a single site. Cold site retains copy of data for DR protection.

Site Definitions

- Active - Could also be referred to as a hot site. An active site is exactly what the name implies. The site is actively servicing user connections.
- Warm - A warm site typically has all of the services built and running. The services are ready to take over user connections through a short failover process.
- Cold - This type of site does not have any of the EUC services running. The necessary services and data are being replicated to the site waiting for recovery.

Active / Cold

The approach of one site being active or hot and the other site being cold, has been around for decades. One might be say this is the historical approach to DR. In this alternative, the organization is running all of its EUC services and infrastructure out of the active data center. The cold site is simply there as a replication target.

An organization can build different levels of capacity at the cold site. This could be a simple as a mirrored 100% capacity. That way, if the active site fails, all services and users will be failed over to the cold site. Once the recovery process is completed all users would be able to re-connect and work. Another approach is to only build something around 50% of capacity. In this approach the organization feels that not all of their users would be able work and may be sent home anyways. The logic is to only build enough capacity to mirror what the organizations global DR strategy is.

I am not sure that everyone would totally agree with the smaller capacity design decision in today's world because many of these EUC services do not rely on backend enterprise applications to provide value. For example, there is plenty of work that someone can do in their virtual desktop outside of connecting to a client server or web based application. Other examples would be user data, if you are providing an enterprise file sync and share (EFSS) solution, users will have a need to access their files.

This approach can be accomplished by using a secondary site within the organization or using a colocation or DR provider as the cold site. Another interesting approach would be to use a DaaS provider as the cold target. There are beginning to be some DaaS providers that are offering this type of solution. You are essentially renting a capacity reservation at a fraction of the cost, should you need to turn on the desktop for a recovery you would then pay a premium. The challenge in the DaaS model is not the base desktop, but the sync of user data; can they also provide recovery of the other services that you provide to your users?

Pros

- Can often be the cheaper method. Some customers may buy minimal infrastructure at target site and plan to expand if an event is declared.
- Easier to architect and understand for many organizations.

Cons

- The RTO time is higher for this alternative.
- The infrastructure at target site is not being utilized.
- There is a long list of recovery steps.

The operational effort for this alternative is typically the highest. There will likely be an extensive DR runbook that needs to be followed to recover the services in this approach. Sure, many of the steps might be opportunities to use automation or scripts, but the end result is a larger effort.

The example diagram below can be used for reference on how the logical view of this alternative might look. The different services each need to be replicated to the cold site. This replication would typically be asynchronous. Essentially, all of the pieces are being replicated to the other site, upon a failure the services would need to be brought online in a specific order. At the top the user connection path is usually accomplished by updating a DNS name so that it would now resolve to the cold site.

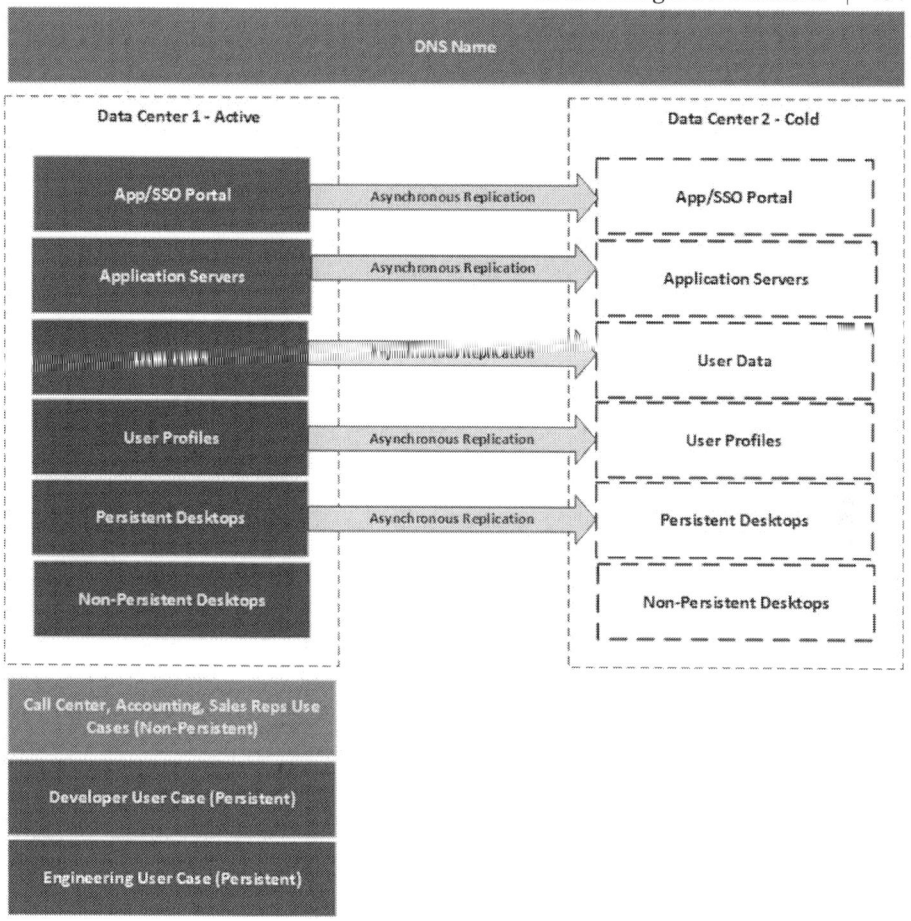

Active / Warm

This alternative is probably where most organizations would like to at least start out. The active / warm architecture occupies the middle ground between old world DR and modern active / active data center designs. This alternative matures what was covered in the previous alternative by having the warm site primed and nearly ready to go.

By calling it warm, all of the EUC services are already built and data is being synchronized between them. The data may or may not be in complete synchronous, there may be a 15 minute difference for example. Within a much shorter time frame and reduced effort the users can be failed over to the warm site.

Pros

- Reduced effort during failover process.
- Some flexibility in where to run use cases.
- Can recover services faster.

Cons

- Price starts to become a constraint.
- A more complex solution to architect.

The diagram below shows the logical example for the active / warm alternative. The data from the active site is being replicated to the warm site. The time within which you want the data to sync is up to your technology or design requirements. This value will also affect the speed at which you might be able recover the services. The data sync direction is typically from the active site to the warm site, but there could be layers, such as user data that is replicated in both directions.

A benefit of this alternative that the cold site alternative cannot provide is the ability to run some of your use cases at the warm site. For example, you can run the engineering use case at the warm site. This works because this use case used persistent virtual desktops, and they have different replication needs. This also works because this use case does not have a heavy dependency on applications located in the primary data center. Under these constraints it allows the organization to use the warm site for this workload.

The failover process here can vary by product and networking approach. It will be important to examine what is possible with the solution you will select. Ideally since the services are built within both sites you would want to be able to use some type of traffic control like global site load balancing (GSLB). This would allow you to create preference for most users to connect to the active site, but if a failure occurs it would direct them to the warm site automatically.

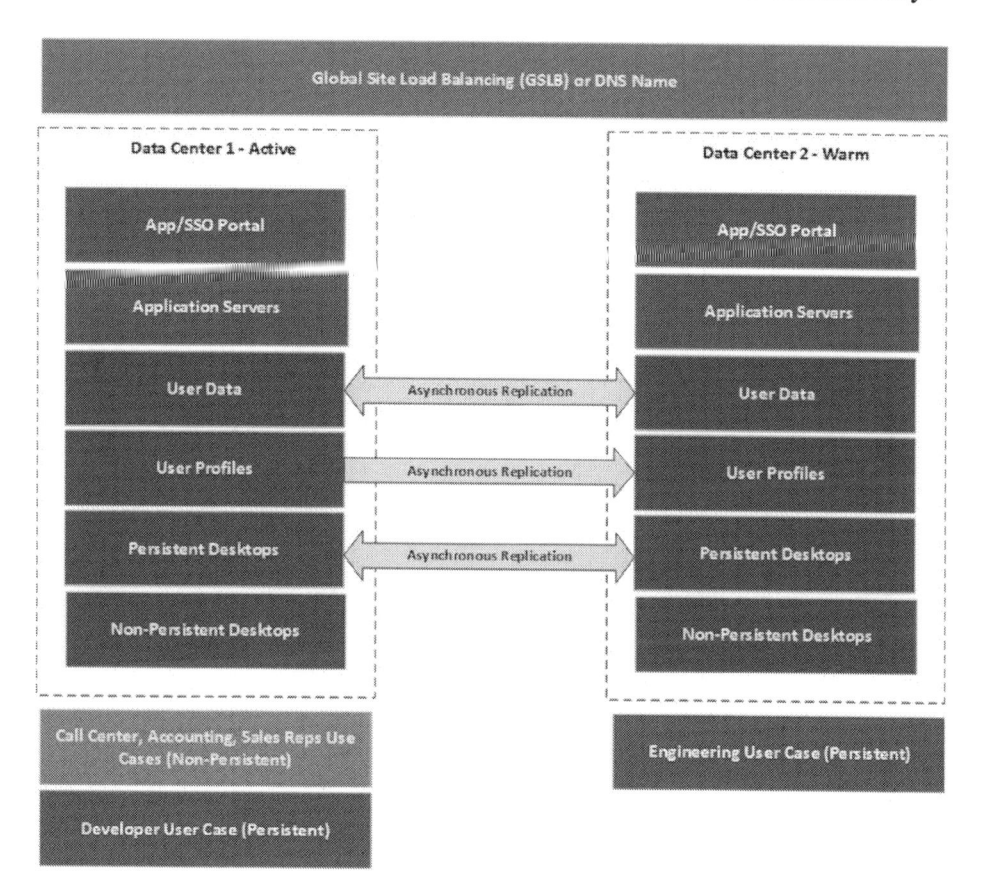

```
                  Global Site Load Balancing (GSLB) or DNS Name

  Data Center 1 - Active                          Data Center 2 - Warm

    App/SSO Portal                                  App/SSO Portal

    Application Servers                             Application Servers

    User Data         <-- Asynchronous Replication --> User Data

    User Profiles     <-- Asynchronous Replication --> User Profiles

    Persistent Desktops <-- Asynchronous Replication --> Persistent Desktops

    Non-Persistent Desktops                         Non-Persistent Desktops

  Call Center, Accounting, Sales Reps Use          Engineering User Case (Persistent)
  Cases (Non-Persistent)

  Developer User Case (Persistent)
```

Active / Active

The active / active alternative is the ideal target architecture that organizations are hoping to achieve. This architecture allows for an extremely highly available set of services. It takes the previous active / warm approach to the next level.

With both data centers being active, all of the EUC services are actively available in both sites. Any unique data must be available in both sites, just in case a user is sent to the alternate site within a short time window. This requires synchronous data replication between the sites, which means low latency and possibly a large amount of network bandwidth.

Another potential issue is that some products might not support this alternative in their current versions. There are some products that do not support multiple data centers, but can have a globally load balanced connection above it to distribute users and allows for the design to act in an active / active manner. Other products or services will only allow for it to be available in a single site. This will cause you to account for failing it over in one of the other alternatives, which makes it a bit of a hybrid approach.

Pros

- Failover is automatically handled by architecture.
- Total flexibility on where to run use cases.
- EUC services should persist, not be recovered.
- (It's super cool.)

Cons

- Price can be a constraint.
- A more complex solution to architect.
- Application performance could be a constraint.
- Might not be possible for all products / services.
- Can have high network requirements.

The diagram below shows the logical example for the active / active alternative. This alternative requires that the services be running in both sites or operate in a stretched manner between the site. The user data must be kept in close sync between both sites. This can be challenging if you do not have enough bandwidth or your sites are too far apart.

Another challenging part of the user data being in both sites is that while it must be in close sync, it must also be writable at both sites. This is not a small detail to overlook. You cannot allow users to be connected to either site based on rules, unless the data is there and writable. So your NAS, file server and/or profile tool must account for this requirement. If you cannot accomplish this, then you are likely falling back to the active / warm alternative.

The biggest driver for this alternative that the others cannot provide is the ability to run any of your use cases at either site. The diagram shows that a single persistent virtual desktop workload is running out of each data center and that several non-persistent use cases are running at both sites. This allows the design to distribute the workloads based on requirements of each use case. These persistent use cases would be replicated to the other site should a failure occur and a failover process would be executed.

The failover process here can vary by product and networking approach. It will be important to examine what is possible with the solution you will select. The expected failover for all services, except the persistent virtual desktops, would be the users upon reconnecting would be sent to the surviving data center. They would establish new sessions and continue working. This would occur because the GSLB would be aware that a site has failed and send connections to the other site.

The persistent desktops would need manual intervention or an automated workflow to assist in the failover. This is because persistent VMs are not designed to exist in an active / active type design. They would be failed over and then imported into the desktop broker, reassigned to the users before being available for connections.

Architecting EUC Solutions

[Figure: Dual active data center architecture diagram showing Global Site Load Balancing (GSLB) across Data Center 1 - Active and Data Center 2 - Active. Each data center contains: App/SSO Portal, Application Servers, User Data, User Profiles, Persistent Desktops, and Non-Persistent Desktops. Synchronous Replication connects User Data and User Profiles between the data centers; Asynchronous Replication connects Persistent Desktops. Use cases shown below: Call Center, Accounting, Sales Reps Use Cases (Non-Persistent), Developer User Case (Persistent), and Engineering User Case (Persistent).]

Cloud services

How might cloud services play into your DR design? This is a great question and would depend on which approach you take. The first would be using a cloud offering as a DR target, this was briefly touched upon earlier.

The second option would be using a cloud or software as a service (SaaS) offering to supply one or several of your EUC services. Let's think about this for a minute- if you use Box.net for your EFSS option or AirWatch as your mobility option and choose the cloud managed version these offer built in resiliency. These both break the internal multi-data center model that has been discussed. Cloud services have their own protection measures built-in will not need to be replicated between your sites.

You will, however, need to fully understand their availability and recovery model. What would happen if one of the services has an outage in a zone or region that affects a set of your user base? Will they notice or will the services re-direct them to another zone? This is part of the attractiveness of a cloud service, but should not be assumed to work that way.

Today a few of the EUC services that have been discussed could be purchased in this fashion, while others would be much less attractive by not offering the same experience that you can get by building internally.

Do You Still Need Backups?

With all the persistent vs non-persistent talk, you are probably wondering does one need to back anything up? The other statement typically that is heard is, "We don't backup desktops today." These are both valuable points, and that is something that needs to be figured out as part of your design.

Let's address the "we don't backup desktops today" topic first. While most would agree this is pretty common, what you are probably missing is that end users are hopefully protecting their data in some fashion. They might be keeping copies in more than one place, on a USB stick for example. Advanced or smart users are using a desktop backup product like Mozy or Carbonite. The point is that since they are in possession of the device and data they can, choose to back it up or not.

If an organization is going to centralize the user's point of access for their daily job, then the design team needs to examine the requirements again. If the use case is using a persistent virtual desktop and there is data and applications being stored within the VM, then there may be a need for it to be backed up. This will have to be vetted for each use case, but since you have given them a persistent desktop there is probably important data and apps in it.

On the non-persistent virtual desktop approach, you do not backup desktops. Period. What does need to be backed up is the master image. Hopefully you use a few of them and back them all up. Since the desktops are designed to be disposable, there should be no data within them that is valuable.

The other parts of the solution that include infrastructure servers, applications servers, session hosts, application layering volumes, user profiles, user data, etc. need to be backed up with your standard backup strategy. If a server fails that is providing one of the services, the operations team will need to be able to get it back from the backups. There will be high availability built into the design, so as long as this happens within a reasonable amount of time everyone should be good.

Summary

As part of your project and use case requirements defining the disaster recovery needs is important. Having well defined requirements around DR will be used in developing your strategy, working through your design and even how the solutions are implemented.

Different products have different levels of maturity when it comes to making DR easy or challenging. You will even find out that of the three alternatives discussed in this chapter only a subset of them may be realistic based on product choices. There will always be a way to provide DR, but you may have to make compromises in the timing or method of recovery.

[13]
Networking

For mobility and EUC architects, the network is sort of like the power company. You need them to get things done; if they are down it affects a lot of things and makes for a very bad day. But, you do not really want to deal with them; you just want it to work. With that said, the network design and services are going to play a critical part in your design. All of the services, applications, and user data will all be dependent on internal or external network connectivity to be available and performing well.

This is going to require you to think about what the network can offer you that may help or constrain your design. Also, you will need to be able to provide a detailed list of what you will require from the network in terms of services, networks, and bandwidth. They should be involved throughout the design process where it makes sense. That way they are not surprised when you are too far down the path.

How Many Networks Will You Need?

Within your design there will be a number of different services and infrastructure layers that will require networks. If you are a smaller shop, many of these may be able to just blend in on existing networks. If you are deploying more than a few hundred users, you are at the size that you will quickly benefit from having dedicated networks for the different parts of the design.

Some of the services will not have large pools of IP address that will be needed. Application presentation servers, however, can eat up a large number based on the user count, and virtual desktops are the biggest consumer of IP addresses in this type of solution within the data center.

Let's focus on thinking about the networks for virtual desktops in your design first. Depending on the size, you may get away with having a single network for all of your VDI, or you may need a network for each pool of desktops. You want to maintain control when just requesting a separate network for everything within your design. There are a few things that will drive you to consider when to combine things into fewer networks and when you will benefit from further separation.

This is where you are going to want to involve the networking team in the discussion as you will need to learn what their current standards are within your data center. As an example, do they only create /24 networks within the data center or are they open to smaller or larger networks based on your requirements? Just to refresh the size of different networks so the next example makes sense, a /24 network has 256 possible addresses. A /23 network has 512 and a /22 has 1024 addresses. There are many more combinations, but these are some of the most common that a typical organization will have in a data center.

255.255.252.0 — A /22 sized network provides 1024 available addresses.

255.255.254.0 — A /23 sized network provides 512 available addresses.

255.255.255.0 — A /24 sized network provides 256 available addresses.

Now if you have four pools of 50 desktops each you could request their own /24 network for each pool or simply combine them all into a single /24 network. There are two things that you should consider: first, is there any security reason that you would want the desktop pools in different networks? Is there a requirement to limit access into or out of one of the desktop pools for compliance or external user access? If not, then a single pool is looking like a better option. The other thing to consider is initially the four pools would be consuming 200 of the 254 possible addresses in the single /24 network. You will not get all of the 254 addresses because the network team will hold some back for routing and other services.

What do you expect the growth to be for those four pools? If you start with 200 and you think that within the next year each pool could grow by 10 desktops, then you will be reaching the maximum of the single network. This would be a good reason to use two /24 networks or if you expect the growth to be large and fast then depending on the final size of the pools you may require a network for each.

What if you will have a large pool with around 1000 desktops? Will your network team create a /22 network for you or can you use multiple smaller networks? The answer to this is you could do either. Though, you should verify with your desktop broker vendor to ensure that they support multiple networks within a single pool. In the end, you are trying to use as few networks as possible, while still accounts for requirements and expected growth.

1000 Desktop network alternatives

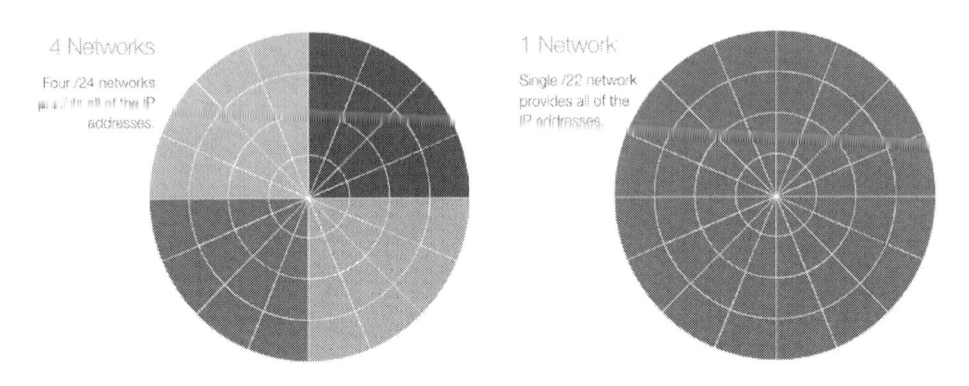

4 Networks
Four /24 networks provide all of the IP addresses.

1 Network
Single /22 network provides all of the IP addresses.

Typically, you are going to place the virtual desktops on their own dedicated networks, while the server VM portions like the brokers, file servers, and other management pieces can be in shared networks or a single dedicated network. An exception to this would be when using Citrix PVS desktops breaking down into smaller networks is recommended. Just be sure to understand the path of communication between the management VMs and the desktop VMs, so that you know how the traffic is routed and if there are any firewalls in the path.

Network Monitoring

Monitoring is covered in more detail in Chapter 14, but the point must be made here also. Within your design there are a number of areas that you will need to be able to monitor network traffic for performance, capacity, and troubleshooting. The user session network monitoring is typically covered in the EUC focused tools and while it is very important, it is only part of discussion.

While you are meeting with the networking team, learn what their capabilities are for monitoring traffic at the WAN connection points, as well as if they have any ability to report on the amount of network traffic from your hypervisor hosts. If you invest in a good performance monitoring tool for the virtualized environment, it should be able to provide you network details at the host, uplink, and VM levels. These are the exact points that you are going to want to be able to look into when troubleshooting and issue or planning for future upgrades.

What are Your DHCP Needs?

When it comes to DHCP addresses in an EUC design, the main topic to be aware of is address availability to non-persistent desktops. Setting a proper DHCP lease time- if it is set too long, you may run out of IPs during certain refresh operations.

To start, no matter which vendor's non-persistent method you are using, you are going to want to shorten your DHCP lease time as low as possible. So that the addresses become available again shortly to the pool for when virtual desktops are refreshed. If you run out of IPs in your pool, the desktops using that network will be refreshed, but will be unable to connect back to the connection broker and will be unavailable to the end users. It is also a good idea to have some amount of buffer built into your pool design to account for issues, even as much as 10% buffer can help avert unseen issues.

The other important detail to account for in your design for DHCP is to create or utilize a highly available DHCP solution. If you are using a network appliance, you should request that it be highly available so that a single node cannot create a complete DHCP outage. If you are using Windows as your DHCP server, the newer versions of Windows Server are able to be configured in a failover cluster to create high availability for DHCP. There are different options on how the cluster distributes load and fails over scopes. The point is that you are not relying on a single server. Should you lose DHCP, you would be faced with sessions being unavailable should they auto refresh on logout or are refreshed by an admin who was unaware of the DHCP issue.

Network Latency

The definition of network latency is how much time it takes for a packet of data to get from one designated point to another. It is typically measured by sending a packet that is returned to the sender; the round-trip time is considered the latency. In EUC solutions, the network latency is often the problem that is most recognizable by end users. Meaning, if network latency gets too high and crosses a certain point, end users will notice and complain. There will also be a higher point at which the service will become unusable.

Back in the use case definition phase, you identified the requirements of which you should have gathered information about the locations the users would be connecting from. This should provide you with data about what locations, the user counts, and network performance data, such as bandwidth and latency estimates. This will help you calculate what the expected user experience would be like, and whether you need to recommend any upgrades to a site's connectivity.

For application presentation and virtual desktops the following numbers are some very generic and vanilla values. Each vendor will provide different data or argue for or against another. This is simply there to provide a rough order of magnitude and allow you to determine your own capabilities.

<50ms — Should provide normal happy user experience.

50-200ms — Users will notice the added latency but still very usable.

>200MS — Users will be heavily affected by latency resulting in delayed user experience.

When it comes to network latency, the lower the better the user experience will be. As it goes higher, the experience will continue to be adversely affected. If your users fall into the less than 50 ms, they will have a normal well performing user experience. The middle group that is in the area between 50 and 200 ms of latency will still have a very workable user experience. Obviously, the lower end of that range is much better than the upper, but still very viable to present remote sessions to sites with that amount of latency.

Once you cross above the 200 ms of latency, the sessions are going to be affected heavily by the latency. History has seen organizations present sessions to users across the globe, and has success even above 300ms of latency. Once you pass 300, though it is going to go downhill very fast. The sessions are going to be very delayed. Adding more bandwidth cannot fix the latency issue caused by the great distance the data must travel.

Network Bandwidth

The network bandwidth portion of the design can be confusing to many organizations and architects. There are a lot of questions including; what values to use? How do you find out the values? Where should one be concerned with bandwidth at? Network bandwidth in an EUC design is not an easy thing to quantify. The fact is you are going to have to start with industry averages and work towards real data from there.

The first place to start is to research what the estimated user session bandwidth requirements are for the vendor that you have selected. These would be different between Citrix and VMware, for example. They should also offer a few different user classifications which may roughly translate to some of your use cases. The classifications will be something like knowledge worker, basic office worker, and developer. Each of those should offer you estimates on average and peak requirements. You can use these estimates and build a table with each of your use cases, including user counts, and apply what you feel is the closest estimate of bandwidth for each use case.

This will give you a very rough guess on what your requirements might look like. From here you can then look at the different layers within your design to see if there is anything that immediately sticks. You should then look towards gathering real data from your use cases. The only real way to do this is through actual testing. For this you would need at minimum a small test environment with all of the applications to test the use cases that you want to collect data on. You then need a small sampling of users from each use case so that they can perform several days of work in the virtualized environment. You can now gather details on the actual data from real user access to update your calculations.

The following are three examples of looking at bandwidth at different layers within the greater design. These are some major points and will be ones that at minimum need to be looked at. For the example it will be using some made up data that will be based on a single use case with 1000 users and they typically use 150 Kbps of bandwidth and can peak to 200 Kbps.

Data Center View

The first look at the bandwidth example will be for the entire 1000 users in the deployment. This is a data center level view that includes both local and remote users. At this level one should be looking at the infrastructure layer within the data center. This view of things is looking to see if there is anything you should be concerned with at the compute layer. Will you have enough bandwidth at each server or if you are using a blade architecture will there be enough bandwidth to each chassis or pair of management devices?

With the session requirements for the sample use case, and the number of users, there would be nothing to worry about. The total estimated bandwidth would be 200 Mbps, if you assume that a 100 VMs to host density that would equal 10 hosts in the design. That 200 Mbps would now be split between 10 hosts at 20 Mbps each, which is a fraction of what today's 1 GbE and 10GbE connections are capable of.

User count	Traffic (Kbps)	Peak Traffic (Kbps)	Total (Kbps)	Peak Total (Kbps)	Peak Total (Mbps)
1,000	150	200	150,000	200,000	200

Within the data center, there would need to be use cases with much higher bandwidth requirements before one would start to get concerned. The mix of higher bandwidth and blades is the most common architecture to be mindful of. Depending on the architecture of the blade solution you select, you may have to adjust your uplink configurations to ensure there is enough bandwidth after you finish your calculations. With rack mount servers all having dual 1 GbE connections at minimum and 10 GbE increasingly becoming the standard it would be very rare to be bandwidth constraint on rack mount servers.

Remote Connection View

The remote connection is the spot where organizations are typically most surprised. For the 1000 user example, this part will assume that 50% of the users work remotely. It does not matter if they are working from one of the organizations remote offices or from home- these connections are all external. This view is going to help set expectations on what the bandwidth requirements will look for the WAN connections.

When you are thinking of what a single session requires for bandwidth that seems very minimal. For remote connections, though, when hundreds of users are needed, the number gets large fast. In the example here, there are 500 remote users with the same estimated values. This results in 100 Mbps of bandwidth needed. That number is not insane in today's world, but there are probably not a lot of organizations that just have an extra 100 Mbps available on their WAN connection.

User count	Traffic (Kbps)	Peak Traffic (Kbps)	Total (Kbps)	Peak Total (Kbps)	Peak Total (Mbps)
500	150	200	75,000	100,000	100

Depending on the size of your design and your organizations connectivity, you should typically expect that there would need to be bandwidth added for these remote connections. You will work closely with the network team provide them details on what the expected average values and peak values will be so they can plan accordingly in their network design.

Remote Office View

This last example is similar to the previous remote session example, except that this one is focusing in on a single remote office location. The previous example accounts for bandwidth on the data center side. You also need to ensure that each remote office location will have enough bandwidth to accommodate the number of sessions at that site. This is probably the level that is most bandwidth constrained in most customer environments. Typically, the current network design allows for general internet usage and application connectivity back to the data center. Though there has never been a need for this level before. This usually results in many remote locations not having enough bandwidth currently and would require a bandwidth increase.

The example here is for a site with 50 remote users using the same estimated values. The estimated value is 10 Mbps for this remote site. Will the allow current connectivity have enough space to accommodate? In past projects, the remote site requirements often leads to a difficult discussion about if the extra bandwidth is worth the benefits, or is there even the option to get this much bandwidth. There have been several organizations that have dozens of remote locations and many of them are in remote rural locations that do not have good connectivity options.

User count	Traffic (Kbps)	Peak Traffic (Kbps)	Total (Kbps)	Peak Total (Kbps)	Peak Total (Mbps)
50	150	200	7,500	10,000	10

A final thing to consider when thinking about bandwidth is the estimated user session values. There can be tasks or work done that creates traffic that would be external to the user's remote session that still needs to be accounted for. An example of this would be remote printing and file shares. If a remote user is connecting to a desktop session in the data center and prints to a printer next to them at the remote location, that traffic will be outside of the VDI session. A similar example would be the same scenario, but the user is accessing files that are located on a file share at the remote location. Either of these operations can result in traffic that is very minimal or can be pretty large if the operations happen often or are using large amounts of data.

You will not be able to fix the printing traffic since the printers need to be near the users, but the file share location is something that you need to visit in your design. The desire would be to move the file share to the data center also, but if there are users that will not be virtual that use it locally you have to evaluate which affects the most users positively or negatively by centralizing the file share.

Load Balancing

Within your EUC design there are sure to be multiple needs for load balancing services. You will need to provide high availability at every layer in all of your services where possible. This is typically done by building multiple broker servers, as an example, and placing them behind a load balancer. They will share a common virtual IP (VIP) address and a single URL address to make reaching them easy and predictable. Within load balancing, there are local and global options. Your design may require both of them. The local option is used for load balancing two or more servers in the same site, while the global option works in conjunction with the local flavor to share the single VIP and URL across multiple sites. This provides additional options for handling load and failures between sites.

Most admins are familiar with load balancing and how they can be used to increase availability. Within your design, as part of the process, you will need to identify all the parts that will be load balanced and what the requirements of each will be. Each vendor and product will have slightly different requirements for how it is setup with the load balancer, and sometime the settings vary based on load balancer vendor.

Depending on the EUC products or vendor that you select as part of your design, there may be additional benefits in selecting a specific load balancing vendor. A good example of this is Citrix has far deeper integration with their NetScaler line than other load balancers. While VMware has built the tightest integration with F5 for their products, it still works with others for standard load balancing. Research what the different load balancers might be able to offer as far as services when design for this layer of the network.

Network Firewalls

Typically, you are not doing a lot of firewall design as part of an EUC solution, although with VMware NSX growing in popularity the ability to virtual segment VMs is proving to be popular. You can learn more about how NSX fits into an EUC design in Chapter 16 on security. You will typically need to account for whether there will be any firewalls that will sit between any of the services you build in the data center, and are there any between internal users and the data center. If either of those are you, then you will need to provide a list of ports and paths that will need to be open for the different services that users will be accessing.

The other firewall function that is almost always part of these designs is for external access. The desire for your external users to be able to connect remotely to the EUC services that are being deployed is a must. You will not want to have to require them to VPN into the corporate network to use these services. They should be able to point to an external URL and get access to all of the services they are entitled through via their login credentials.

For this to happen, there are usually network devices or virtual servers that need to be placed on the edge of your network so they are accessible externally. This is typically known as the DMZ network. The security and network teams will have special requirements that you will have to meet. You are going to need to document the traffic paths with the source and destination ports so that they can configure the firewalls appropriately to allow the traffic to reach the different services. This is something that you want to spend a good amount of time researching so that you provide a complete list. If you miss ports and you have to keep going back to the team for changes, and this can slow the deployment down to a standstill.

Summary

Within EUC designs both small and large there will be a number of network related decisions that must be made. You hope that your network is able to compliment your EUC design rather than be a constraint to it. Either way you should feel more confident in the details that you are seeking and the data that you will need to provide the network team. Oh and it does not hurt to buy those network guys some donuts every now and then.

[14]
Operations

As you are designing your shiny new EUC environment, you should always keep in mind that someone is going to have to support it on a daily basis. The decisions made should account for the operational requirements and effort to ensure that a highly supportable design is created. The goal should be to create a solution that will be easy to support and still maintain a high quality of user experience.

Your desired state EUC environment will likely have hundreds or thousands of users consuming services on a daily basis. This level of demand will require some well-defined operational processes and tools to be in place. There is also the question of who will support this new EUC wonderland? An EUC environment that comprises of several of the services that have been discussed in this book includes a lot of different skill sets.

In this chapter were going to cover some of the tools, features, and skills that you need to evaluate when planning for your EUC environment.

Reporting

The need for being able to generate meaningful reports will be high. Different parts of the organization will be requesting data from the EUC environment from usage to security. The operations team will look towards reports for capacity and performance data.

By centralizing your EUC services, the ability to collect and report on data is more possible than in the past. As part of your design and evaluation process, you should be determining what your reporting requirements might be. You can also gather reporting requests from the other teams that will be involved in the support of the EUC environment.

Once you have gathered the reporting requirements from the greater project, you will need to determine if and how you might be able to supply the requested data. Each of the products that you ultimately select will have some level of reporting built into them. The built in reporting is usually somewhat limited, though. The next question is will you require a specialized reporting product to provide the data that your team's need?

The common answer to that question is increasingly yes. The market is seeing a large adoption of specialized EUC reporting based products by organizations. These are purpose built for reporting on end user environments and deliver features and data that built-in reports or general reporting tools cannot provide.

The good news is that this product space is growing and maturing quickly. In the past couple of years there were just a few products that were focused in this area, and they were working hard to increase awareness of this need. In the past year, the market has welcomed multiple new and existing vendors that have released products in this reporting space. The following is a list of the leading and new products in EUC reporting and monitoring space.

EUC Reporting Tools

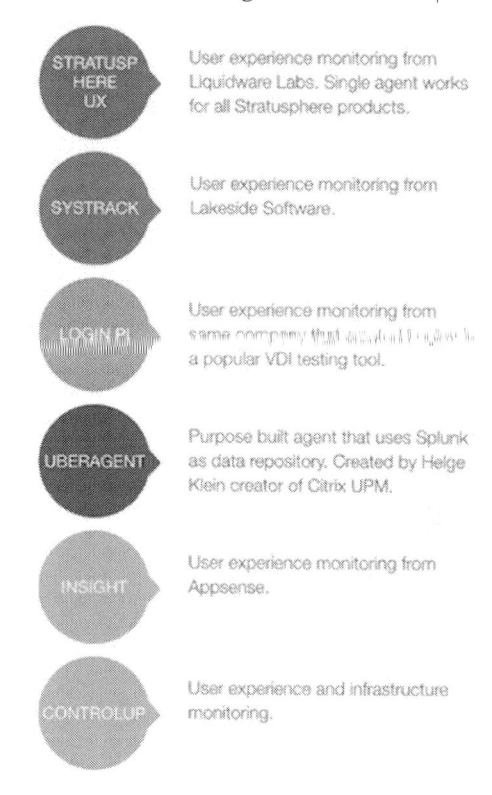

- **STRATUSPHERE UX** — User experience monitoring from Liquidware Labs. Single agent works for all Stratusphere products.
- **SYSTRACK** — User experience monitoring from Lakeside Software.
- **LOGIN PI** — User experience monitoring from same company that makes Login VSI, a popular VDI testing tool.
- **UBERAGENT** — Purpose built agent that uses Splunk as data repository. Created by Helge Klein creator of Citrix UPM.
- **INSIGHT** — User experience monitoring from Appsense.
- **CONTROLUP** — User experience and infrastructure monitoring.

The following is a short list of some of the reports that are available in many of these products. These types of reports will be very useful in the planning and managing of your environments.

- Who is logged in currently?
- Who was using a specific session on a specific date and time?
- Application assignment versus usage.
- Session statistics.
- Last login date.
- Which apps require elevated access?
- Login duration.
- GPO performance.
- Application identification.
- Application launch times.

- Compute and Storage support.
- Endpoints (deploy and manage).
- Help desk.

Monitoring

The reporting needs were just covered for an EUC environment, and next will be a look at monitoring. Today these are two important needs and are most likely going to be provided by two different products. There is not a good product that can provide you the level of monitoring and reporting that organizations will need in one solution. You may be asking, what is the difference between reporting and monitoring? There will be product in both categories that do some of both features. The main difference is how well they do covering the virtualization and infrastructure layers versus the end user experience part. Today the reporting tools do a better job on the user experience data points, but you will need to put in effort to identify points important to your organization, and how to utilize them.

The monitoring product will need to provide coverage of the infrastructure, virtual infrastructure including the VMs and hopefully the EUC infrastructure. To get complete coverage of a Horizon Suite deployment today, it would require vRealize Operations (vROps), and Stratusphere UX, or a similar product. In this example, vROps would cover the infrastructure monitoring, vSphere monitoring and Horizon monitoring. Stratusphere UX will provide the reporting features and fill in many holes that vROps cannot monitor currently. This combination properly informs your operations team to proactively monitor the EUC services for issues, performance, and capacity. If you are deploying a Citrix focused EUC design on vSphere you are likely to deploy vROps and Citrix Edgesight or Citrix Desktop Director.

EUC Monitoring Tools

VROPS — vRealize Operations for Horizon offers monitoring solution for virtual layer, infrastructure and Horizon layer.

VMTURBO — Provides virtualization monitoring and recommendations on improving performance and capacity.

FOGLIGHT — Dell Foglight offers virtual infrastructure monitoring and multiple plugins allow application monitoring.

SOLARWINDS — Provides virtualization monitoring with options to add-on network, application and other features.

XANGATI — Provides virtualization monitoring and VDI broker monitoring options.

CONTROLUP — User experience and infrastructure monitoring.

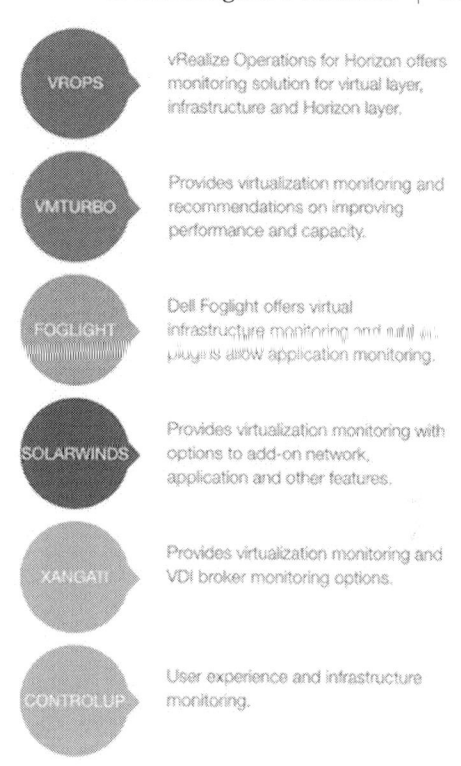

Monitoring is focused on real-time stats or recent data, while reporting will be more historical in nature. In evaluating your monitoring product, you will need to examine closely what types of data it will be able to provide on the different layers of the solution. Does it have the ability to collect stats and data from the physical infrastructure? Are there plugins, management packs, or add-ons to the product to allow other vendors to send data to for a single monitoring location? This is one thing that makes VMware vROps attractive, many vendors have created management packs allowing admins a single tool for the bulk of their monitoring needs.

Operational Items

Besides the monitoring, reporting, and closing help desk tickets there are some other operational items to discuss. The goal is to not focus on most of the tasks specifically contained within each of the products, as these are fairly well defined. They are also already contained within the product. The focus is on tasks that must be accomplished manually or with a well-defined process, or may require a third-party product to provide the features needed.

It should be a high priority for the operations team to develop a process for creating the base images. These base images will be used for app servers, virtual desktops, and RDSH servers. The goal is to have a documented and repeatable method for deploying the base OS. Then be able to customize the base install by making all necessary changes for performance, stability, and security. There will be separate requirements for the sever images versus desktop images and they should be documented.

By having a well-defined and documented process, you will have a solid foundation for your image maintenance. Once your images are in use within the environment, you will typically keep multiple version of them for rotation and backups. As updates are applied a change log should be kept so that the team understands any changes and updates made to the image. This will be crucial for future upgrades, and may come in handy during any troubleshooting activities.

Another task that can be overlooked is the ability to shadow user sessions. The support team is going to need to be able to shadow users at different times to assist with issues and provide assistance. When preparing your design, you will need to understand if the desktop vendor that you selected provides this function in their offering, or if you will require a separate product to provide the shadowing functionality.

EUC Team

Once your EUC design has been deployed, the ongoing operations and support of the environment must be planned for. Leadership and the project team will need to identify the skills required for supporting your design and what team(s)

Architecting EUC Solutions | 165

will support it. There are two common approaches to the team question. The first option is to stay with the status quo and stay with a siloed approach. The second option is to form a new EUC focused team. The skills required and team discussion will be examined in the following sections of this chapter.

The following is a list of the skill sets that would be required to support a modern EUC design as discussed in this book.

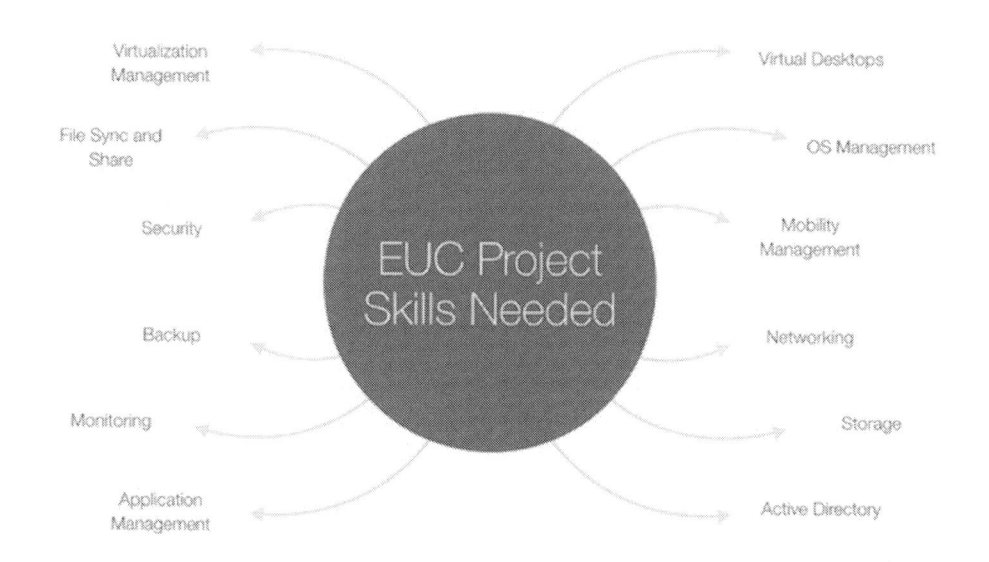

EUC Project Skills Needed:
- Virtualization Management
- File Sync and Share
- Security
- Backup
- Monitoring
- Application Management
- Virtual Desktops
- OS Management
- Mobility Management
- Networking
- Storage
- Active Directory

Application Management - The applications as explained in several earlier chapters are critical to the design. Due to this fact, you are going to need a variety of application related skills on your team or available to your team by request. You will need applications packaged, and they will need to be updated and patched. Depending on how you manage applications there will be some sort of application presentation or layering to setup and manage. Also, applications will typically need some sort of monitoring, whether for availability or performance. The monitoring team will typically monitor the application while the EUC team will monitor the presentation or layering part of the application.

Virtual Desktops - Other roles cover layers that affect desktops, but virtual desktops (VDI/SBC) are more than just a Windows OS running in a VM. To manage this part, the skillset is part desktop administrator and part virtualization administrator. Then add in the desktop brokering layer and this is something new to most organizations.

Virtualization Management - Within any EUC environment there are going to be many VMs, whether they are virtual servers or virtual desktops mentioned just before this. With these, the team that manages VMs and the virtual infrastructure for performance, capacity, and general admin duties is crucial.

OS Management - This would be primarily focused on the deployment of client versions of the Windows OS. You will need skills that include being able to build and maintain a repeatable deployment process, along with providing OS support, security configurations, and the ability to create, update and track versions for image management.

Mobility Management - This is a skill set that most organizations do not possess or they are very immature currently. As you begin to make mobile devices first class citizens in your environment, you will need the ability to manage devices, data, and applications- all while setting and controlling policy to protect your data.

File Sync and Share - This is also a very new skill for most organizations. The ability to store, sync, and share files via a cloud or on-premises based service similar to Box.net or Dropbox, is in high demand. Much like mobile management, there are not a lot of skilled people in this area. Organizations need to develop skills or hire people that are capable of implementing and supporting this service and the policy based management that is part of securing data.

Security - Nearly every organization has a dedicated security person or team, or at least someone that wears this hat part time. This skill set is typically not needed on the EUC team, though it is required as part of the greater project team. The project team will need to work closely with security to develop access policies and restriction, SSO, and other policies.

Networking - The famous network team will be an important part of the project team. There will likely be networks to setup and firewall ports to open. A project like this has lots of bandwidth considerations, whether locally or on your wide area network (WAN). Networking also includes monitoring network performance and remote access support.

Active Directory - If this was not obvious already then maybe were doing a bad job. The project team will have a number of requests to the team that manages Active Directory. There will be user accounts, security groups, organizational units (OU) and group policies to create and manage as part of your design.

Backup - Hopefully the majority of your virtual desktops are designed in a non-persistent fashion, and you only need to protect the images. There will also be server VMs, user profiles, and data that will all need to be backed up. The project team will need to work closely to ensure they achieve the level of protection required for the SLA's.

Storage - This is just another infrastructure service that the EUC services will need to consume. Within your EUC design, there could potentially be different types of storage utilized. These may be all managed by the storage team, or there are many organizations adopting modern hybrid flash storage or hyper-converged infrastructures. These modern storage options are simple to manage and can often be managed by the new EUC team.

Monitoring - For monitoring this likely will have duties split between teams. Typically, legacy server VMs, network, storage, and compute monitoring will be done by a traditional monitoring team. While the EUC focused tools covered earlier in this chapter are likely to be used and managed by the new EUC team.

Team Building

If you are deploying all of EUC services that have been discussed in this book, then your organization may be lacking experience in several of the required skillets. This is because many of these will be new to most organizations. They will need to take one of two approaches to close the skills gaps. The first approach is to train the existing team members on the missing skills. This can be time consuming. You may also lack capable or willing employees for this approach. The second option is to recruit external resources that possess the skills already or can be hired with the intent that learning these new skills is their priority.

Once you have acquired all the necessary skills you will still need to figure out how you assemble them into a team. The following two options look at doing nothing by keeping your siloed teams versus building a new EUC focused team.

Status Quo

This approach to supporting your EUC design assumes that your organization has a standard team organization structure. This typically means that each major technology stack has its own team. This is also referred to as a siloed structure. Each of the teams focuses specifically on their part of the environment, and only interacts with other groups when a request is asked of them or within a project. With this type of organization, the result is that it typically takes longer to complete tasks and collaboration is reduced.

Following the siloed approach, one should expect that the existing desktop team would likely support the endpoints and the Windows client OS in the VDI VMs. The VMware or virtualization admin team would likely support the virtualization hosts that the servers and desktops run on. There would be a storage team to manage the store; a network team would manage connectivity and so on.

The new skills that would need to be learned or acquired externally would likely be contained within a new silo. An example could be a new team that would manage the mobile management solution. They would be focused on managing mobile devices and the policies.

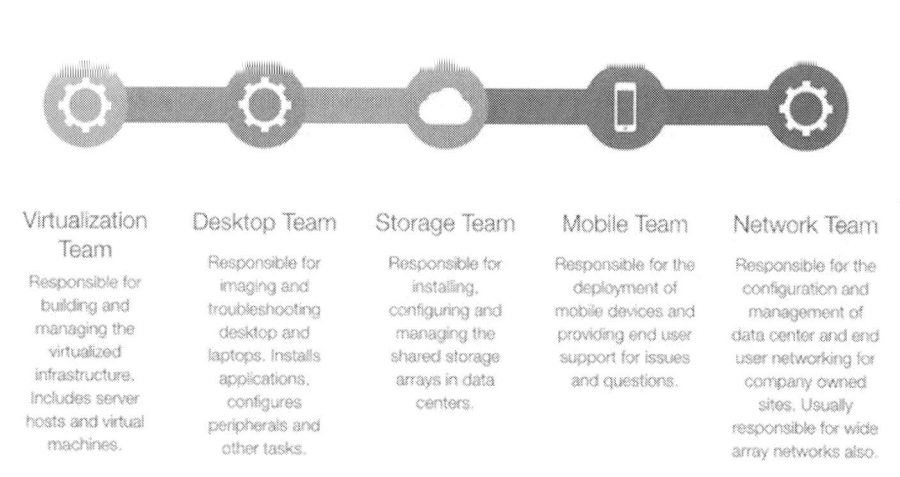

Status Quo Team Method

Virtualization Team
Responsible for building and managing the virtualized infrastructure. Includes server hosts and virtual machines.

Desktop Team
Responsible for imaging and troubleshooting desktop and laptops. Installs applications, configures peripherals and other tasks.

Storage Team
Responsible for installing, configuring and managing the shared storage arrays in data centers.

Mobile Team
Responsible for the deployment of mobile devices and providing end user support for issues and questions.

Network Team
Responsible for the configuration and management of data center and end user networking for company owned sites. Usually responsible for wide array networks also.

Now imagine if there is a major outage or just a complaint about end user experience that needs to be researched. This is likely going to be involving a minimum of five different teams within the IT organization. Each team will have its own agenda and may apply a different level of priority to the request. The typical result is that this approach lowers satisfaction of the IT team members, and can negatively affect the users' perception during support requests.

Create Something New

This alternative operates on the idea that you are building a completely new set of services that makes up your new EUC services catalog. To support this, you will need a team that is specifically focused on the EUC environment and its users. This approach does not necessarily mean that the EUC comprises of every skill set that was listed earlier in this chapter. The team would combine the skills that are tightly coupled with managing the services of the EUC design.

Do not assume that this means that you must run out and hire a new team of people, meaning that your costs are going to surge. A great place to start is by identifying people from the existing siloed teams that would offer valuable skills to the new team. This means that you can go employee shopping on the current desktop support, VMware admin, and deployment teams. You are likely to be able to find the people you are looking for to build your design and support it once completed.

There are teams that will remain in their siloed existing teams that simply provide infrastructure resources and support to the EUC environment and team. These would be different parts of the infrastructure such as security, network, storage, and others. These are the teams that will need to have a close working relationship with the EUC team, but do not need to be members since they are also involved in support their environments for other parts of the business.

By building your team from existing teams that poses the necessary skills you will have a team that has all of the necessary skills. Over time the different members on the EUC team will be cross-trained so that they can support multiple or all of the services within the environment. This can happen organically or via structure to ensure the knowledge is transferred. If some team members are new hires to fill gaps they will learn the tribal expertise from other members, while helping train others on their specific skills.

Architecting EUC Solutions | 171

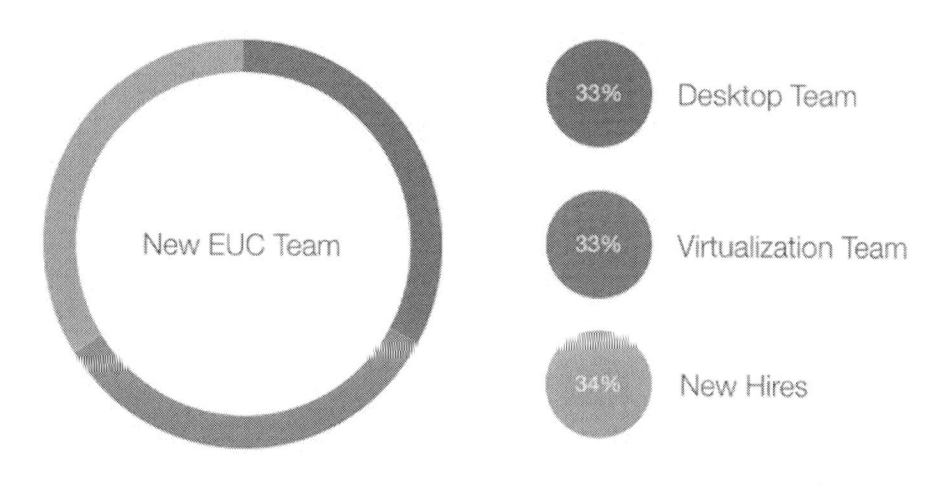

New EUC Team

33% Desktop Team

33% Virtualization Team

34% New Hires

In the end, you will have a focused team that is dedicated to supporting your new EUC environment. They will understand the requirements of your users intimately, and will be prepared to address issues and be proactive in their support approach.

Depending on which infrastructure is selected to provide resources to the EUC design, there may be additional opportunity to collapse the skills within the EUC team. An example of this would be selecting a hyperconverged (HCI) storage vendor to provide the compute and storage resources for the design. These HCI vendors have created products that are very simple to deploy and manage. This would allow the infrastructure to be managed by the EUC team without the need to rely on the external storage and compute teams. A collapsed approach would allow the team to arrive at the root cause of issues in a shorter period and the ability to perform maintenance on the environment would be simplified by having all the skills within the team.

There is no simple answer to the team structure that works for every organization. Recent history is starting to show that the EUC focused team approach yields a better support experience for most organizations.

Summary

In summary the operations part of launching an EUC project can be just as complicated as designing and building the solution. If you don't get your toolset right and properly plan for the support team aspect they can both cause you to be ill prepared and end user experience can suffer affecting your success.

[15]

Infrastructure

The infrastructure portion of your design can be exciting to some, and completely boring to others. In your eyes, the infrastructure should be the foundation on which you will build your services. But it's also like electricity and water, everyone counts on them, but they should just work when the faucet or switch is turned on. Someone has to care for them, but not the customer.

Without a stable, highly available, and high performing infrastructure below your design, you will be facing any number of challenges during the deployment and operational phases of your EUC project. This re-enforces the reality that the infrastructure is very important, but spending a large portion of your time on the infrastructure is a black hole. It should be the belief of leadership that architects and engineers need to be focused on providing the EUC services and applications, rather than managing the plumbing.

When designing infrastructure for EUC projects, there are several important factors that should be focused on in the design process. By using these factors along with the organizations requirements, one is better able to consider what the architecture alternatives are going to be. The following are the main factors that should be considered when evaluating architecture alternatives and vendor options on EUC projects.

- Entry point

- Scalability
- Performance
- Monitoring
- Capacity

Entry Point

The entry point can often be a make or break decision on a project or the architecture alternative that is selected. This is how much infrastructure and cost will it take for an organization to start the deployment based on different starting point sizes.

If the project is planned to reach 10,000 users when fully deployed, and the starting deployment phase is to start with 5,000 users, the organization is probably less inclined to be shocked by starting costs. The reasoning is that depending on the type of infrastructure that you select the per-user cost may not begin to make sense until you have deployed a few thousand users.

The flip side of this is that you plan to deploy those 10,000 users but only intend to start with 500 users and scale up at a steady pace over the project time line. You are going to look closer at the cost of the initial infrastructure deployment at this size over taking a larger first step. The per-user cost at this size can hold steady as you increase the deployment or it can look really skewed in the beginning, due to a larger starting infrastructure spend.

While I am not a fan of a per-user cost as a factor to determine your infrastructure costs, you are going to be asked about this when trying to sell the project to the business or justifying your infrastructure selection to leadership. This alone should not sway one's decision in one direction, but if you choose an alternative that has a higher up-front user cost, you need to be prepared to explain the details. Be able to defend the decision by explaining how the costs will eventually level out or significantly lower as the environment scales. The following diagram is a sample of the two scenarios that have just been discussed.

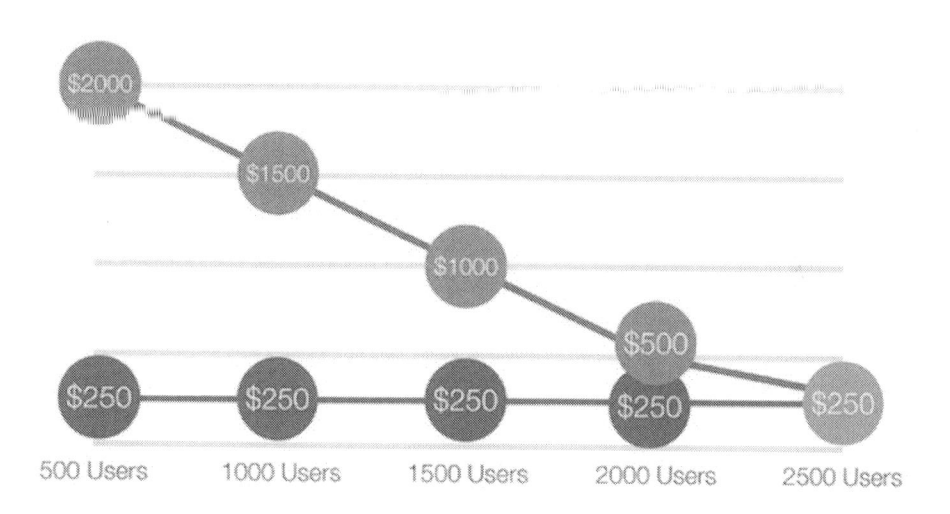

Entry Points

[Chart showing two scenarios across 500, 1000, 1500, 2000, 2500 Users. One line declines from $2000 → $1500 → $1000 → $500 → $250. The other line remains flat at $250 across all user counts.]

Scalability

The scalability of architecture alternatives is an important factor when evaluating their viability for the project. You will need to understand what the starting size options are for the different alternatives. This loops back to the entry point topic that was just covered. Will the alternative easily allow the design to start at a potential small size that may be required? Or will the organization need to purchase more infrastructure than would be needed to satisfy ones starting size and not be able to utilize all the resources until the project grows into it?

Aside from how small of a scale the alternative can start with, you should carefully consider how large the alternative can scale too. If you want to start at 500 and still be able to scale to the 10,000 users, what will the alternative look like at both ends of that spectrum? Will you be happy with the low or high points or both?

The scalability topic is not just a storage discussion, it also holds true for compute, networking, and possibly other layers within the design. If one adjusts the configuration of the servers in order to achieve a smaller density of VMs per host server, how might this affect the choices when the project scales? A good example would be if the initial host design starts with 128 GB of memory per host and the final choice is 256 GB or larger, one needs to ensure that the right size DIMMs are used in order to allow for the configuration to be scaled in the future. If the wrong choices are made to save costs, it will end up affecting the density due to constraints or costs more in the long run since you may have to throw away the DIMMs that you were unable to re-use.

A popular alternative is how a solution is able to start small, as well being able to scale to the largest point. You cannot ignore all the points in between either. Depending on how you scale the deployment, there could be many scaling points in between the start and finish points. You should be looking for something that is going to allow you to easily scale in buckets of user counts that the project identifies, while not outpacing the deployment timeline and capabilities. An example of this would be the ideal scaling bucket size for the project may be in increments of 500-1000 users, if the architecture alternative chosen scales lopsided you will need to understand how this affects the costs and deployment.

Performance

The performance of any architecture alternative is always looked at closely, and must be able to meet the project's requirements at any phase of the project. This can be a tricky path to walk with some alternatives. If you scale some solutions down small to meet your minimum starting user requirements, you may be sacrificing the performance of a solution if they are unable to scale linearly. You also do not want to have to make compromises in the architecture to reach this small starting point that may affect the overall maximum performance options of a solution. Just spend the time to ensure how decisions you or a vendor are making, may affect the solution on the starting and finally states.

Within an EUC, solution you typically have many different performance requirements. The desire would be to select an architecture alternative that is flexible enough to meet all of the performance requirements within a single option. Whether you are providing several types of EUC services, or just focused on VDI, there are going to be multiple performance needs that must be accounted for. Understanding how each alternative is able to or not able to meet these requirements with a single solution, or will it require multiple options to meet the performance needs, will heavily affect your evaluation and design process.

Capacity

When thinking of capacity, the discussion is similar to the performance one. There are a number of very different capacity requirements within EUC designs that will need to be provided. The solution will call for running server VMs, desktop VMs, applications, user profiles, and user data are typically part of this type of architecture. Each of those layers within the design have very different capacity requirements. Some of them use large amounts of data that typically deduplicate well, while other portions such as user profiles, and data are smaller amounts of data per user but multiplied by thousands of users, turns out to be a large portion in the end.

Something that was a larger problem in years past was purchasing too much or too little capacity, while trying to achieve the performance levels required. I'm closely looking at architecture alternatives during the design phase to see how they will be able to provide required capacity while the focus is on ensuring the minimum performance requirements are also met. The alternative should not give 2-3 times or more the capacity while just meeting the performance requirements. or the opposite would be to have to purchase additional performance in order to meet the capacity requirement. The ideal solution is one that would allow enough flexibility to scale performance and capacity at a similar rate so that neither gets too far out of pace from the other.

In the past, a lot of debate and issues have been caused by this very topic. History has seen many organizations get themselves into performance and capacity planning trouble by scaling the capacity faster than performance. Just because the solution had 5 TB of free space, does not mean that it is able to scale by another 500 users, or whatever the metric seems to indicate. This very scenario may cause the performance to suffer greatly. Falling into this trap can trick admins that do not have a solid understanding of how the solution scales, and where the tipping points may be. Also, it can easily confuse leadership into thinking that capacity equals room to grow.

Monitoring

Not unlike the other topics discussed, monitoring is very important and most often overlooked. When it comes to monitoring your infrastructure in an EUC environment, you are typically going to be focused on the performance aspect. You need to easily be able to understand what is normal and when there is an active issue.

Using the monitoring should be easy, but still provide a wealth of detailed information. This is not easy for many manufacturers, so you should be looking closely look at what the monitoring experience is with each alternative that you are evaluating.

Another requirement in is the ability to provide performance monitoring at the VM level. It is 2016, and the majority of infrastructure vendors still cannot offer this level of visibility into your VMware environment. The ability to quickly look at the storage layer and determine if the storage performance issue is at the global scale or if it is isolated to a host, group of VMs, or just a single VM is not an option any longer.

By managing storage performance at the VM level, you can use a similar approach to managing the CPU and memory performance of a VM at the host level. As an admin, one wants to know if a VM is temporarily using additional performance or if they are a regular consumer of more storage performance than the typical users. This will allow one to understand when there is a spike, and when you should be looking into something further to identify the issue.

Building Blocks

A building block is a predefined set of infrastructure that maps to a specific amount of resources or number of users. This approach is one of the best ways to approach infrastructure design when working with an EUC design.

By using this approach, you can develop an architecture that offers you a predictable cost, performance, and capacity scaling model. When determining what your building block size is, you are going to be looking at what increments you are going to want to scale users and how your infrastructure selection can accommodate the choices. For instance, you may want to scale users in increments of 200 users, but your infrastructure choice does not scale in that small of increments well. This may force you to scale in larger increments of 500 or 1000 users. If your infrastructure choice scales in large blocks you can choose to scale to mesh with that or just accept the fact that your infrastructure costs will not scale in the same way that your user deployment blocks will. This simply means that you would be purchasing infrastructure in blocks of 1000 users and only be deploying in groups of 200 users.

This is not the end of the world. It does make the costs of the virtual desktops or user sessions look expensive when purchasing the large block to deploy a smaller amount of users. This eventually evens out if you do deploy all of the planned users. It is important, however, to communicate this to business leadership.

Building block style architectures are helpful in any design project. EUC deployments always have common chunks of users and use cases that have similar characteristics, and are deployed in groups, making it a grand candidate for building block style. To continue with the example of a 200 user block size, by understanding the resource requirements of 200 users one can ensure that the block of infrastructure is able to provide everything that those users require.

If each user requires 15 IOPS and 30 GB of storage capacity, along with 2 GB of memory and 200 MHZ of CPU, you then know that the building blocks must provide 3000 IOPS, 6 TB of capacity, 400 GB of memory, and 40 GHZ of CPU. As you design the building blocks, you can contain additional resources. None of the blocks can be below those values, you also do not want to wastefully include too much extra of any of them if possible in each block that cannot utilized.

With this approach and granularity in the design, one can now scale the environment in groups of 200 users. This allows for a slow and steady approach, and provides predicable values that we can plan around for deployment, performance, capacity, and costs. If you wants to scale faster and in larger quantities, you just drop in multiple building blocks at once.

Lastly, the building block approach has proven successful because experience has shown a majority of customer deployments like to start with a smaller deployment and scale up from there. This start small and grow method allows organizations to not have to invest a large amount of capital up front, and allows them to learn lessons and gain experience and the deployment grows. This approach also aligns perfectly with the pod based designs recommended by EUC and infrastructure vendors.

The next section covers the different types of infrastructure architectures available today and how each of them support or do not support the building block approach.

Infrastructure Alternatives

In today's market place, there are really three primary architecture alternatives that customers commonly evaluate for EUC solutions. The alternatives are Build Your Own (BYO), Converged Infrastructure, and Hyperconverged Infrastructure. Each of these alternatives will be explained in the following sections.

Build Your Own (BYO)

The BYO infrastructure alternative is really just what the title implies, the architect or team is going to independently choose products that they like or they feel are best of breed. This alternative results in a significant increase in the upfront planning and research period, as the team must evaluate each product separately and how they may or may not work together.

You also have the option in this alternative to select and follow a reference architecture that a vendor has published for the type of solution that you are building. These reference architectures will typically be published by a single vendor and focuses on their product suites- after all they want to sell their products. These reference architectures can be helpful in saving time and reducing a little bit of risk, but they do not always apply to your design, use cases and environment.

At minimum a BYO alternative for an EUC-based design is going to contain compute and storage resources. You are likely able to use existing network connectivity so that it will not be a component of this alternative. The following diagram illustrates a simple example of the parts of a BYO alternative. With the flexibility in scaling the costs typically would be fairly predictable; the only exception would be on the storage side. Depending on the maximum size of your design and the storage choice made you may require multiple storage arrays or appliances. As you scale the storage and need to add a new storage array or appliance the cost will spike at those points.

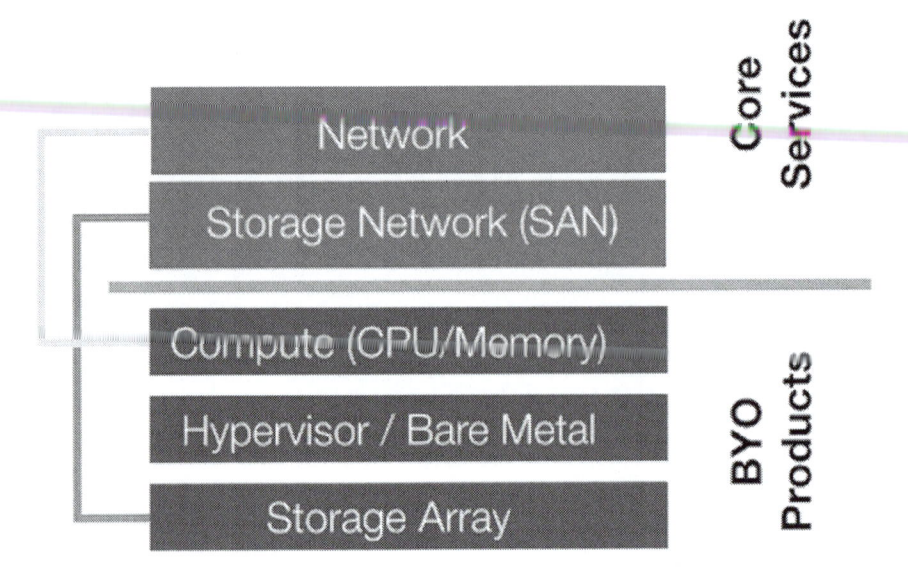

```
                    Network                    | Core
              Storage Network (SAN)            | Services
              ─────────────────────────
              Compute (CPU/Memory)             |
              Hypervisor / Bare Metal          | BYO
                 Storage Array                 | Products
```

Bring Your Own (BYO) Infrastructure

Anytime that you are assembling a number of products from the same vendor or multiple vendors without prior experience, there is extra risk. You will be unable to ensure the performance and reliability of the solution until the actual infrastructure is purchased and deployed in the architected manner.

If you can accept the unknowns and additional risk, the BYO alternative does provide you with maximum flexibility. Since you are able to make nearly any vendor and product decision that is capable of working together, this allows you to stay with existing vendors you have good luck with, while moving to new vendors in areas that you seek change in.

A BYO alternative is able to scale the compute and storage resources independently. The only limits to the scaling method or the maximum size would be a constraint of the individual product choice. Since the products are purchased separately, there are no minimums that or set amounts that the products need to be scaled in. This allows flexibility in trying to account for the building block approach mentioned earlier.

Converge Infrastructure

A converged infrastructure alternative is an architecture that was brought to market about five years ago. Converged infrastructure offerings typically offers the same products that might be selected as part of the BYO alternative, and package them together into a productized solution. This means that a converged infrastructure vendor will include compute, storage, and networking in their offering. Typically, most converged infrastructure offerings will contain products from multiple vendors and be included as part of a single converged infrastructure offering or a vendor can offer all of the layers of a converged infrastructure offering from their product line.

The following diagram illustrates a simple example of a converged infrastructure alternative.

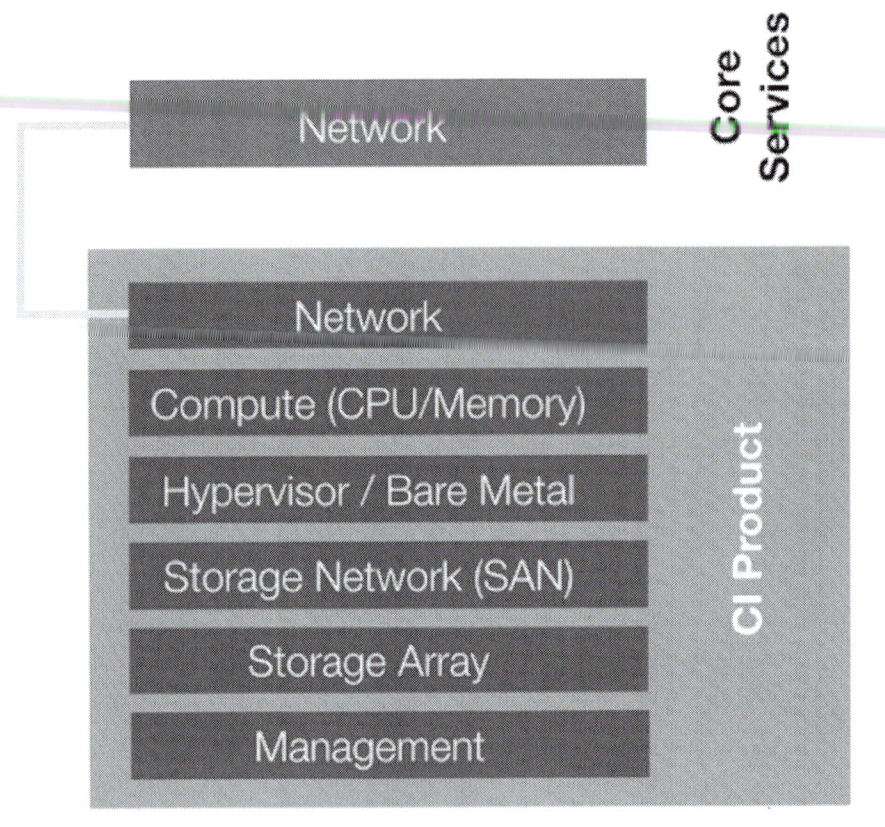

Architecting EUC Solutions

Converged Infrastructure

Diagram elements: Network (Core Services); CI Product containing Network, Compute (CPU/Memory), Hypervisor / Bare Metal, Storage Network (SAN), Storage Array, Management.

The attraction of a converged infrastructure offering may be that you are able to purchase familiar products that have been packaged into a single solution. This can be thought of a reference architecture that can be purchased as a product. Depending on the converged infrastructure product that you evaluate, the product may or may not offer any additional convergence than if you purchased the products separately in a BYO alternative.

Most converged infrastructure vendors and products will usually offer you the ability to purchase all of the infrastructure parts in a single product SKU. The converged infrastructure vendor should be able to offer you single call support for the entire converged infrastructure solution. This means that the converged infrastructure vendor can support all of the products within the solution. This is an added benefit as it allows the customers to work with just the converged infrastructure vendor and not have to involve multiple vendors in the troubleshooting process.

As part of most converged infrastructure product offerings, there is also the added benefit that there are a limited number of products that are offered within the solution. This allows the converged infrastructure vendor to pre-test and validate all of the parts and pieces to ensure they work properly together, removing much of the risk that was in the BYO alternative.

Today even after five years of converged infrastructure products being sold in the market, there has been little done by the converged infrastructure vendors to simplify the management of these products.

With the converged infrastructure offerings including the same products that are available in the BYO alternative, you will typically manage both alternatives in a similar and disperse manner. This alternative may combine the purchase and/or some of the products. It does not usually converge the daily operational management of the solution, though.

A converged infrastructure product should be able to scale the resources within it independently of each other. This would mean that you can add just compute, although there may be some minimum increments at which you can scale the compute. The other resource that would be scaled in a converged infrastructure offering is the storage, and this will be heavily dependent on the type of storage solution select as part of the converged infrastructure offering. A converged infrastructure product will have a maximum size, meaning that it will have a limit on the number of servers that it can support and a storage limit that will be based on the included storage array.

These scaling limits of a converged infrastructure offering are typically fairly large, but at some point as you scale the resources within the converged infrastructure product you will hit the maximums. To continue to scale your design at this point will be to purchase an additional converged infrastructure product and begin scaling it. This will cause large peaks in infrastructure costs at different points of the scaling process, depending on the maximum size of your design.

Hyperconverged Infrastructure

The hyperconverged architecture was introduced to the market place about five years ago and has been available for purchase for around four years, depending on the vendor. The hyperconverged name is one that was given to this architecture approach by an industry analyst.

True hyper-converged architectures are achieved by converging the compute resources, storage resources, and management layer into a single product. It is possible to deploy a hyperconverged solution in a BYO or reference architecture method, but to be truly hyperconverged the product must include a hardware appliance as part of the solution.

By including a hardware appliance as part of the product, the vendor can now include the management of the infrastructure along with the other resources that are being converged in the product. The following diagram illustrates a simple example of a hyperconverged infrastructure alternative.

Architecting EUC Solutions | 187

Hyperconverged Infrastructure

A truly hyperconverged product will offer a number of benefits that the other reference architectures are unable to offer. The following items are several of the primary benefits of hyperconverged infrastructure.

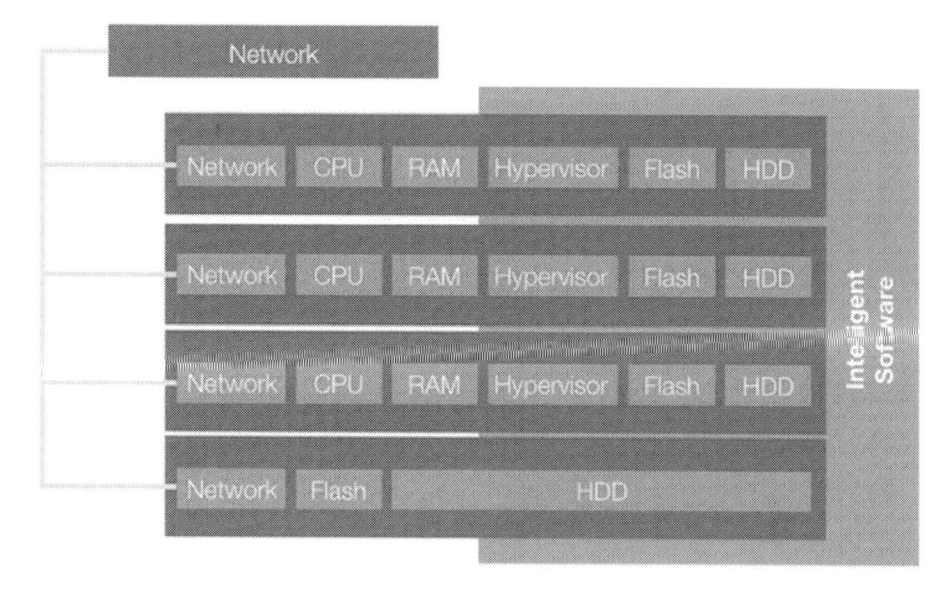

- **Simple Install** - The leading hyperconverged infrastructure products should install nodes within minutes not hours and the process should be highly automated.
- **Easy to Scale** - Just as with the install you should expect that the product is as easy to scale up or down. Previously, the building block approach was discussed and this is exactly how hyperconverged infrastructure works: start with a certain amount of nodes and then add additional nodes as your design scales up. The addition of new nodes to the environment should happen easily through the management interface and only take a short amount of time.
- **Modern Management** - To truly evaluate the management experience to modern levels, the product cannot focus of legacy storage details such as LUNS and other values. A modern management interface must focus on the

VM as the point of management. An admin must be able to understand how VMs are performing, how much resources each is consuming, and if any have any events or errors. Also, the ability to easily pull reports based on VMs is a must. The interface should be clean and simple and be accessible from nearly any device easily.

- **Extensible** - In order or infrastructure to become back of mind it must be able to integrate with other parts of the solution easily and be able to be controlled programmatically. This requires the hyperconverged infrastructure product to offer an API and possibly another method such as PowerShell. With an API you will be able to automate the communication and control between products to further reduce the effort and increase the accuracy of the environment.

Performance was left out of the hyperconverged infrastructure benefit on purpose, because everyone expects a modern hybrid or flash based solution to perform great.

Most organizations need to understand that hyperconverged infrastructure is less about performance and all about creating an infrastructure layer that is simple, efficient and allows your teams to stop spending their time turning knobs and elevate their skills to provide additional value to the business at the automation or application level.

Storage Requirements

With any EUC design there are a number of different storage resource requirements that will exist. The design will need to account for server based VMs, user data, and finally VDI. The VDI storage requirements will be the most demanding with the environment, and also are the ones that cause most VDI projects to fail or suffer from bad experience.

For this reason, the storage portion of this will be focused on the needs of the VDI service of the solution. The needs of each virtual desktop can often seem

Architecting EUC Solutions | 189

small an insignificant. When you combine them into large groups as the storage scales, however, the performance demands can easily overwhelm storage that was not properly design to meet these needs.

If each of the virtual desktops is going to average 15 IOPS and one expects to have 2000 concurrent users, then that works out to be an average of 30,000 IOPS. That number is pretty large. and could overwhelm the average storage array. You cannot simply design the storage solution to meet the average I/O of the environment, it must account for the peaks.

A virtual desktop workload is very different from the other types of workloads run within the average enterprise data center. As virtual desktops are very spiky in their I/O nature. This means that something as simple as opening an application like Outlook for the first time in a session can generate upwards of a 1000 IOPS for that one user session. That is far beyond the average 15 IOPS that we discussed earlier.

VDI IOPS

MS Update — 2500 IOPS
MS Word — 1000 IOPS
Acrobat — 800 IOPS
MS Excel — 1400 IOPS
15 IOPS

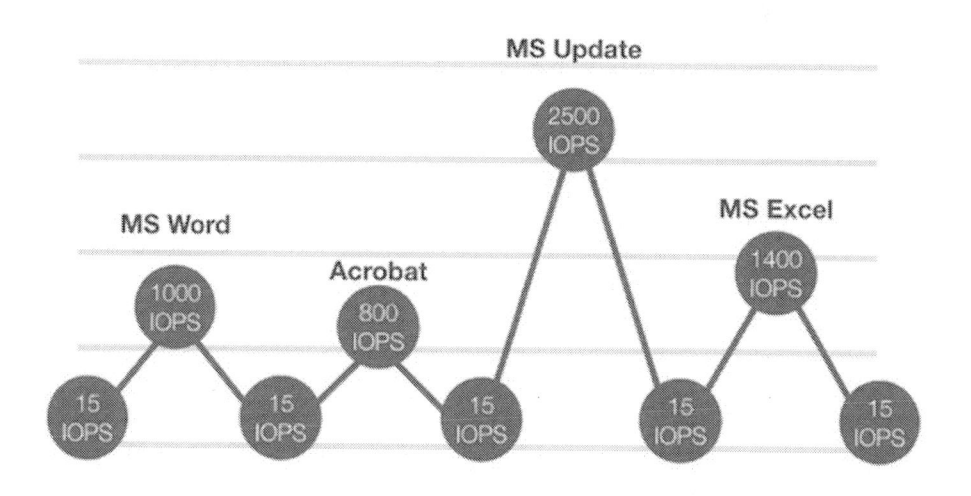

Other deployment and operational items, such as patching and environment refreshes, can also create a tremendous spike in IOPS, and will affect performance if not accounted for and planned accordingly. If you deploy another 50 users and had to create virtual desktops for them, then that action can create a significant spike in I/O. Patching a large number of users can also generate large amounts of I/O. For these reasons, you will need to account for maintenance operations into your storage architecture for peak IOPS.

There are a number of ways to architect VDI solutions with full clones or shared image presentation and each can have different effects on storage requirements in both capacity and performance. If you are using full clones for virtual desktops each consume additional capacity and storage with deduplication will be important. Full clones must all be patched independently which will increase the I/O during those operations.

The shared image approach that Citrix offers with MCS or PVS, and VMware with linked clones, presents different I/O challenges. By nature, these shared image approaches require less storage capacity since the parent image is shared and each virtual desktop is only consuming a smaller amount of space for its unique data. The shared image has different performance requirements that the typical VM. This image is now used by hundreds or thousands of virtual desktops, and must be able to generate large amounts of IOPS. If the shared image is a bottleneck all of the virtual desktops using it will be negatively affected and user experience will be bad.

Taking in these considerations for peaks and different types of VDI architectures, you must select and design a storage solution that is capable of meeting the peak demands of the environment. To understand the storage requirements for your design, you should be performing a desktop assessment on your existing physical PC environment as discussed in Chapter 5 earlier.

A final thought on VDI storage requirements is that desktop workloads aside from being very unpredictable in the I/O side of things is that they are also very write heavy. Unlike many server workloads that are mostly reading data and serving it up to users, desktops are typically spending more time writing to disk and this is more intensive to the storage array than reads are. A typical server workload might be 80% reads and 20% writes, while a virtual desktop workload might be the opposite with 80% writes and 20% reads. While evaluating your storage choices, be sure to pay close attention to how the storage solution buffers and commits writes versus some large promise that it does an excellent job at caching commonly read blocks.

Storage Types

Within the storage industry there are a number of different types of storage. The primary storage alternatives available today are legacy tiered storage arrays, hybrid flash arrays, and all flash arrays. Each of these alternatives takes different approach to how they provide performance and capacity to workloads. Within each of the alternatives, vendors take different approaches in building their offerings, so a brief explanation of each is listed below.

Legacy Tiered Architectures - Think of this alternative as the legacy enterprise arrays that have been used for server based workloads for the last 10-20 years. These are typically dual controller based architectures. Within the last decade, these have been modified to allow for multiple tiers of performance and capacity disks to be included in the architecture. These different tiers of disks are there to try and service the capacity and performance demands of disperse workloads. There are two options in this approach: you can design for performance by creating dedicated pools of high performing disks for a workload. This can be very expensive and limiting. The other option is to try and take advantage of tiering that was added to this architecture to ask the array to promote or demote blocks of data based upon its demand. The trouble with this auto-tiering is that it often takes too much time to make those decisions for VDI workloads.

Hybrid Flash - These hybrid storage arrays are modern architectures that we designed to efficiently use a combination of flash drives and spinning disks.

192 | *Architecting EUC Solutions*

There are a number of vendors that take different architecture approaches on how they use these different types of capacity and performance in their arrays, but the end result is similar. They are able to offer impressive performance from a smaller amount of flash while still providing a large amount of capacity by storing data on the large spinning disks in the array.

All Flash - As you can assume from the name of all flash the storage array in this alternative is entirely made up of flash based storage. There are many different types of flash that can be used within these storage arrays. To me, a modern all flash array must be a product that was designed specifically to take advantage of the characteristics of flash storage. This means that the OS and file system were specifically designed with flash in mind. There are some products available that have taken a legacy array design, and simply replace the spinning disks with all flash. While this is still faster than its older counterpart, the product was not designed for this purpose.

All flash storage arrays are going to be very fast with only one level of performance in the product. To ensure that the array can also provide the capacity required for the design at an affordable price, you are going to be looking for arrays that offer deduplication and compression as features. While nearly every modern all flash arrays are easier to manage than their legacy counterparts, they do not always offer the same ease of management and per-VM management that many of the hybrid flash offerings do.

The last 2 years of experience has shown the only architectures that are a fit for a modern VDI designs are hybrid and all-flash storage architectures.

These architectures are capable of providing the performance required for VDI environments, and also offer the modern management experiences discussed earlier. VDI workloads are very unpredictable by nature and if your storage solution must wait to make storage decisions or promote blocks to a caching tier, the performance demand will be long gone before that happens and the experience will have been negatively affected.

Compute Sizing

When it comes to sizing the compute layer of your design, there are different schools of thought. The first would be the scale up approach, which uses fewer large hosts to provide resources. The scale out approach will use more small hosts to provide resources. The preferred method is some place in between the two approaches, which will utilize two socket hosts, and make them as dense as you can without violating the consolidation ratios that were set as part of the design. For the purpose of this book, the focus will be on helping size the compute resource for your VDI workload.

There are three primary calculations that you will be focused on when sizing the compute resources in your design. They are the amount of physical memory in each host, the amount of CPU clock speed, and the number of CPU cores and the CPU ratio for them. First and foremost, you never overcommit the memory in a VDI design. This is a recommendation to follow closely. Violating this has very little value and will only lead to performance issue in the environment.

The CPU clock speed calculation is going to depend heavily on the details that you gathered in your previous desktop assessment. The reports from the assessment will tell us the amount of CPU that user sessions used on average and peak. The example will use those details along with the memory details from the assessment to make the calculations shortly.

A couple of other vSphere cluster recommendations are to target 80-90% host utilization and always size your cluster for N+1. The 80% host utilization has been a long time VMware recommendation, but VDI clusters can be easily managed into the low 90th percentile of utilization. The second item of figuring for N+1 in your cluster sizing is to ensure that there are enough resources in your cluster that accounts for a single host failure to ensure that all VMs can keep running and failed ones will restart without issue. A single host failure is the most common level of residency, from time to time one will see customers that require N+2 to account for higher SLA requirements.

The final item on the compute sizing topic is the CPU ratio, which specifically focuses on the number of virtual CPUs to physical CPUs (vCPU:pCPU). This ratio is very important because if you go too high with this ratio, you will reach a point where there it a CPU scheduling issue will arise and this will dramatically affect performance and user experience. When a CPU scheduling issue happens on vSphere hosts, the amount of CPU ready time increases and this lets one know that the scheduler is having trouble getting all of the vCPU's scheduled onto pCPU's. This means there the vCPU will have to wait even though it is ready. The CPU ratio is very different for the various types of workloads that are virtualized on VMware clusters. Typically, server and database workloads have a much smaller ratio, while VDI workloads are able to have a higher ratio.

One vendor's CPU is no different than another's CPU when they are both using the same Intel E5 chips. When it comes to VM density for CPU ratios, one vendor is not going to be any better than the next. So if someone is trying to say they can get 50% or double what others are saying you should dig in deeper and see what they are hiding. They are either lying, don't know any better or are using a very small desktop size that you would never deploy in production and you should walk away from them.

The use of vCPUs is not a linear calculation, meaning that one can build a host that has a higher consolidation ratio if all of the VMs have only a single vCPU. When you have many VMs that have two or more vCPUs this will affect the calculations and it's not as easy as dividing by two to account for twice as many vCPU's. The diagram below represents a range that has proven to work with real customer deployments. There are different manufacturers that do synthetic testing that may shower higher ratios. You should be careful with these as they do not always apply to real world designs.

Architecting EUC Solutions | 195

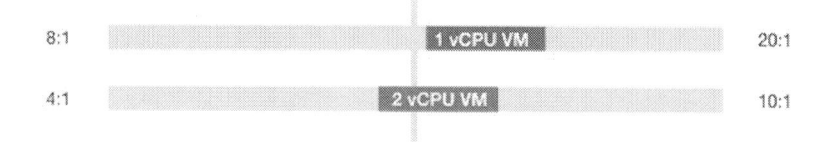

| 8:1 | | 1 vCPU VM | | 20:1 |
| 4:1 | | 2 vCPU VM | | 10:1 |

VDI consolidation ratio is heavily driven by the ratio of vCPU to pCPU. The calculations are different based on the number of vCPU your virtual desktops will be configured with. The chart represents a range that experience has proven to be safe.

The working range that you should operate in normally for single vCPU virtual desktops is between 8:1 and 20:1. This is a large range. Where you should land in that range is driven by different choices- some of which would be how large are the hosts built and what would be the number of VMs per host and the customers comfort with that number.

An example would be a dual socket host with dual 18 core CPUs. This could accommodate upwards of 720 VMs on the high size providing you had the right memory and enough clock speed available. This would scare most customers having that many VMs on a single host. So there are two choices to make in this scenario: first would be to choose a lower density that you are artificially limiting. If you choose the lower end of the ratio, it would net you 288 VMs on the same host.

The second option would be to choose CPUs with fewer cores, but choose a ratio some place in the middle. If you choose 12 core CPUs and use a 12:1 ratio that would net use 288 VMs. This decision is typically a combination of customer feedback, architects' recommendation and infrastructure pricing. There may be a significant cost savings by choosing different physical CPU configurations that will help guide this decision.

The calculations for a dual vCPU virtual desktop are similar, except that you are now dealing with double the amount of vCPUs. The range that you should operate in here is between 4:1 and 10:1 and growing The industry has seen vendors promise higher, but these are driven by real customer deployments. You should use the same decision points as the previous example, just with a different CPU ratio range.

Something to keep in mind is that if you select a CPU ratio in the middle of those ranges, then it allows you the freedom to scale your consolidation density upwards should the environment continue to perform within tolerances. A thing to note is that there is a not have place to configure these CPU ratio's as a setting in vCenter or any other tools today.

These are design attributes that must be declared in your design and become data points that you will need to account for in the management and scaling of your environment. Just as much and memory and clock speed, the CPU ratio needs to be calculated into the decision to add more VMs to a cluster and when to add another host to a cluster to provide more resources.

You can manage the CPU ratio through manual calculations by gathering data or have also seen admins use a PowerShell script that will gather data and present the ratio for you as the output from the script. With a script you could run it as a scheduled job daily to ensure you are not violating the ratio and be in danger on any of your clusters.

With todays CPU core counts the reality is that you will probably be limited by the amount of memory in a host or the number of VMs per node that you are comfortable with before you hit a CPU ratio in many cases.

vSphere Cluster Design

Within an EUC design, there can be a number of reasons for different vSphere clusters to be created. The decision to have different clusters is typically going to be driven by different workloads and cluster size. I will not spend a large amount of time on this subject; the goal is to offer a few recommendations that build on the topics already covered.

First and foremost, if you are building a VDI design of more than a few hundred users, you should be separating your management infrastructure from the VDI workload. This means that all of the management servers, VDI brokers, file servers, application manage servers, and any other functions that are not virtual desktops should be running in a different cluster. Whether the management cluster needs to be one just dedicated to your EUC design is going to depend on how large your environment will be. If the design is smaller, you can run these management VMs in an existing server VMware cluster.

On the virtual desktop cluster(s), you will scale these clusters up to reach a size that is between 16-32 hosts. This range both allows for a larger resource pool to be created for VMs to use, and also pushes organizations to adopter a cluster size that is large than their typical sizes. Recent hypervisor updates allow for clusters to size up to 64 hosts, it will take time for architects and customers to feel comfortable going that large. If the environment is large enough that the host counts would exceed these ranges, then there would be a need for more than one VDI cluster.

Another reason that you would design for multiple vSphere clusters, besides environment size, would be for the different workloads. We already discussed having a management cluster, but within the VDI clusters there are different workloads. Specifically, we discussed the different CPU consolidation details and how different configurations drive different densities. If you have a significant amount of one (1) vCPU and two (2) vCPU virtual desktops, you are going to design a separate cluster for each. This will allow you to manage the CPU ratio differently in each cluster, allowing for an easier to manage design. If you were to blend the different CPU configurations there would be a new blended ratio that would need to be calculated and that just confuses things.

Management cluster

Provides resources to all non-desktop workloads in the design.

Desktop clusters

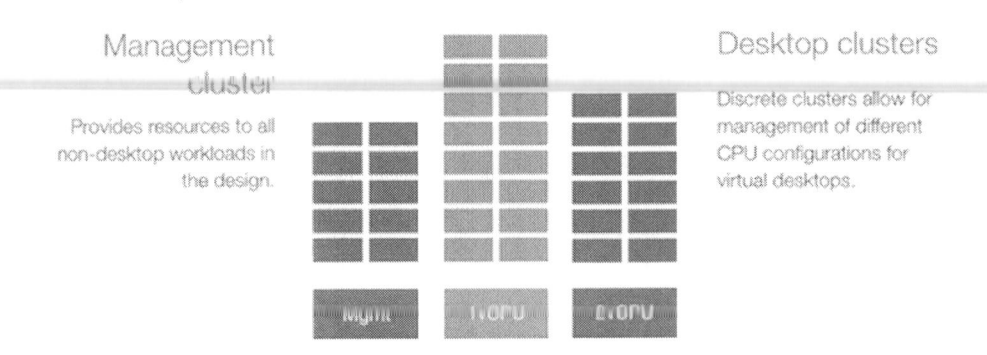

Discrete clusters allow for management of different CPU configurations for virtual desktops.

Summary

EUC infrastructure design and sizing are focusing heavily on compute and storage requirements. While there is little differentiation in compute alternatives and sizing currently, it is still important to define and follow your design choices.

Storage is still an incredibly important part of EUC and VDI designs. Luckily there are a number of alternatives that can provide the needed capacity and performance required. The differentiation will be realized in something other than IOP numbers.

In 2015, the hyperconverged architecture put all other architectures on notice that it is the best alternative for EUC solutions. The gap will widen in 2016 as HCI vendors continue to add features and tighten management stories.

Appendix A at the end of the book includes a sample design sizing exercise on Nutanix infrastructure. This applies the data points discussed in this chapter to Nutanix as an example and can also be applied to other options with minimal effort.

[16]
Security

Security? Who needs security anyways? Is it not only that grumpy guy in the bowtie that always derails project meetings that cares about security? Truth be told, many EUC projects got their start based on the security benefits that the different services or technologies would put into place.

There can be many security related benefits to centralizing an organizations data, and strictly controlling access to it with policies. On the flip side, if not done properly, giving people access to company data from any device without proper security measures can create a worse security position than in the past. Like many of the other design related parts of this book, security is not something to be taken lightly.

Given that on a monthly basis the world now hears about major security breaches at some of the world's largest organizations, you better believe that business and IT leaders are worried a lot about security. For this reason alone, you need to make sure that you are gathering security requirements from your leadership and ensure that if there is a security team in your organization that they have input into your EUC project.

There is far more to securing an EUC design than enabling or preventing user logins. The remaining parts of this chapter will discuss several key topics. This is by no means a complete comprehensive list, but will be a good start to your discussions and point you in the right direction. The topics that will be discussed in rest of the chapter are illustrated in the diagram below.

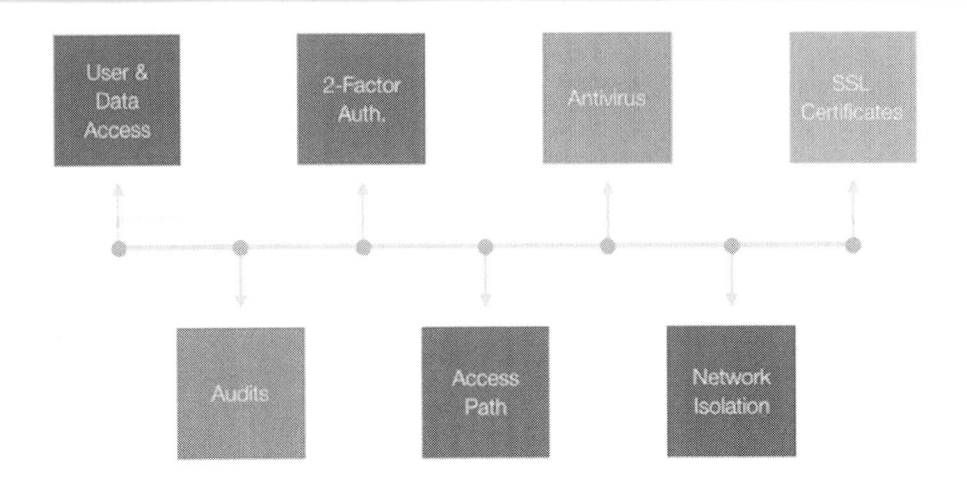

User Access

This probably seems obvious but there will need to be a way to entitle and un-entitle users to the EUC services. In most organizations Microsoft Active Directory (AD) is the authoritative directory that contains all users accounts. Each user will need to be entitled to access to the different services and their user data by enabling their AD account access to these points.

If you are doing any type of deployment of more than a few users, you should be using security groups within AD. AD groups allow you to create groups of users, you can then entitle that group to a service rather than each individual user. This is a time savings over trying to manage hundreds or thousands of individual user accounts. Part of the process to enable users to a service would be to place them into the appropriate AD groups. This will give them access to the services, just by being a member of the group. This is far easier than having to use the management interface for multiple products and then entitling the users account for each service.

Another feature that has steadily increased as EUC has grown over the years is SSO. SSO provides a central point of authentication for users to enter their credentials once. Then the SSO service passes those credentials to the other services in the backgrounds as user access. This allows a user to login once and then use any of the EUC services without having to log into each one individually.

Some of the EUC vendors have already built a portal that operates as a single access point that also serves as the SSO login. If you are using the other services from that vendor, they are likely to support SSO between the products accomplishing your goal of reduced logins. There are also third-party SSO products that you may be able to use with your EUC products. Most SSO products today use Security Assertion Markup Language (SAML) as the open standard for exchanging authentication between products.

If the products you choose support SAML, you will likely have better success in making them work together. Also, the products from EUC vendors such as VMware and Citrix offer SAML support in their SSO products to allow them to work with internet services and other external applications.

Two-factor authentication

With all of the security breaches lately the addition of two-factor authentication seems like a no brainer. The real question becomes how it will affect your design in a positive or negative way. You will need to make sure that the products that you deploy support two-factor, and hopefully the one that you have or want to deploy.

Two-factor authentication provides unambiguous identification of users by means of the combination of two different components. These components may be something that the user knows, something that the user possesses, or something that is inseparable from the user. A good example from everyday life is the withdrawing of money from a cash machine. Only the correct combination of a bank card (something that the user possesses) and a PIN (personal identification number, i.e. something that the user knows) allow the transaction to be carried out.

In most organizations the second factor can be one of many things. It could be a certificate or file that must be provided to a user that is located on the device. It could be an application on a mobile device that provides a pin, or it could be a text message sent to the user's phone. There are many options available for this approach without having to hand out the old expensive key fob that RSA used to provide.

The key is not to authenticate your users to death. You probably only need to enforce two-factor when they are accessing services from outside of your corporate network. Ideally users should also only need to authenticate once for services externally and use two-factor for that. If they have to enter credentials more than once, you will likely hear complaints about that.

Data Access Policies

At this point the book has already talked about entitling users to EUC services and data via their AD account. Beyond the base entitlement, you are going to need to establish more finite policies on what is allowed and not allowed within different parts of the environment. Also, you may allow one use case to perform a certain action, but not allow all of the other use cases to perform the same action. This will be done through the use of policies.

Policies can be created and configured in the different EUC products or through using group policy in AD. Many vendors allow for some policies to be created in there management interfaces and then publish Administrative Templates that can be imported into AD to allow for policies to be established within AD for controlling their products. This allows for a commonly understood method to be used, and will likely provide greater flexibility than the policies that are built into the vendor's product.

The following is a list of some policies that you will consider on whether to allow or deny them to your different use cases. This is not a complete list, just meant to point you in the right direction.

- USB access
- Mass storage access
- Local drive redirection
- Copy and paste to endpoint
- Local printer access

Antivirus

Probably 95% of all virtual desktops are using Windows as the OS. There are some Linux-based deployments, but with limited support from VMware and Citrix this will remain a small part of the market. Let's face it; Windows gets viruses and malware on a regular basis. There are a lot of exploits and malicious code out there, and users do stupid things that allow these to get installed. Because of these reasons you will need to protect your data and protect users from themselves at times.

To do this you are going to need antivirus (AV) protection. The different AV vendors offer a wide set of features for protecting Windows, and this book will not be covering what they all offer. Rather, this book will discuss why there is a need to have AV protection in your design.

In the last few years there have been a few vendors and architects make the statement that you no longer need AV protection if you are using stateless desktops. The argument is that if a virtual desktop gets infected or compromised you can simply delete it, refresh it back to the master image, and everything is clean again.

That really does sound fantastic, doesn't it? Well it is all a pipe-dream, and you should not get sucked into this fairy tale. Let's think about this a bit further. A desktop gets infected and It takes a while before the user complains about an issue. Someone on the operations team eventually determines after investigating that the issue is due to a virus. Someone then makes the call to refresh the offending desktop, and they hope all is well now.

If you think about the nature of how many viruses propagate, they are able to jump from desktop to desktop. Thus, allowing them to infect a large number of machines in a short period of time. Since there was nothing in place to stop the infection from happing in the first place, the desktop was infected. Depending on the type of virus, it was probably able to spread to other desktops before the operations team had time to deal with the originally reported desktop.

The idea of refreshing a single desktop and thinking everything is clean is not very realistic. Unless you are able to determine in a short period of time, and then refresh every virtual desktop in your environment at the same time this argument does not hold much hope. Also, what if physical computers were affected and are then spreading the virus to the virtual desktops? You will need to deal with that if they are allowed to communicate. The point is today just as much in the past you will need to protect your virtual desktops from malicious code.

Depending on which AV vendor you have purchased and which hypervisor you will be using, you will have two possible choices on how to deploy. You can take the historical approach, and deploy the AV agent into the OS and push updates and perform your scans from each OS instance. This is a far more work-intensive approach to AV management. It uses more of the resources from the host servers when performing scan. Even if properly designed and implemented, this approach can have very negative effects on the environments performance during peak usage times.

The other approach if you will be using VMware vSphere as the hypervisor is to perform the AV scans at the hypervisor layer. This is done by using vShield

Endpoint to allow the AV vendor to plug into the hypervisor and have access to the virtual disks of the VMs. You will need to evaluate to see if the AV vendor you are using already supports this or make this an important feature to consider for a new AV purchase.

SSL Certificates

With any of the leading EUC suite offerings from vendors today, there will be a large need for SSL certificates in the deployment. Many of the services have web components to them and securing them with valid certificates is critical to ensuring the security of your users.

Within an EUC design, there will be needs for certificates that can be requested from an internal Certificate Authority (CA) such as AD. These are perfectly acceptable for devices that are members of your AD domain and trust the CA by default. If devices will access these services and are not members of the AD domain, then they will need to have the CA added to their keystore so that they trust the certificates and do not display warnings that can confuse your users.

The externally facing services in your design are going to need certificates from a publicly trusted CA. These CAs are ones that are used to issue certificates to web sites that you visit every day and for stores that use them to secure your purchases. There is a cost to purchase these certificates and depending on your design and the number of services you deploy you may have a need for several of these public certificates.

These public certificates are especially important for devices that are not members of your AD domain and for mobile devices. These do not trust your CA from the internal AD domain, but they do have built in support for many of the top level public CA's. You will want to do some research on which one has the best results with different devices. For example, you may find a great deal on a public SSL certificate from a lesser known vendor. This vendor may be trusted by default on Apple mobile devices, but might not be trusted by default on all Android based devices.

This will cause confusion with your users when they see a warning when trying to access services with the device. You will need to then enable that device to trust the CA that you used to purchase the certificates from. This can be a painful process if there are a lot of devices. You also need to do this with any new device that has the same issue. Most will find it much easier to just spend a little extra money and get your certificates from one of the leading vendors that others have success with.

Audits

Depending on the policies of your organization, you may need to retain desktop data to be looked by security. This might be because you are in a heavily regulated industry, or maybe it is just because a user did something malicious. Either way, at times someone within or external to your organization maybe need to perform detailed discovery on a virtual desktop.

If the desktop is a stateless or non-persistent type of desktop you run the risk of destroying needed data if it were to be refreshed before or during the discovery phase. So this brings up the question, what are your requirements around this level of historical data? The user profile would be captured and retained as part of the user experience, but this would be more around OS logs and other files external to the user profile.

As part of your design and working with security, you will need to identify the requirements for this type of request. If there are none, then you get off easy. If there are some, then you will need to examine the different methods on how to retain this data without restricting your design choices around the desktop methods that you plan to use to delivery virtual desktops with.

There are several options available to consider, you can look at redirecting logs or forwarding logs to a central point. Note this is typically not needed for virtual desktops that are persistent since they should never be refreshed.

Access Path

With the different EUC services that were discussed earlier in the book, the design enable users to specific services and their data without giving them complete access to the data center. In the past, you would typically enable users that needed external access with a VPN connection. This connection may give them complete access to internal networks or a few organizations would go a step further and ensure that there was a profile for different VPN users that would only grant them access to specific networks that they needed to perform their work.

The latter is a more secure approach. By enabling users access to services and data based on their ID, allows you to control their access path. There should be a central point of access and are securing that access with their ID and have applied policies to prevent users from doing tasks in an insecure manor. Using this approach, the design does not need to enable users to load the VPN client on nearly any device to gain open access to the organizations networks.

By funneling them through the EUC access path it only grants them access to the desktop, applications, and data that they are entitle to use and nothing more.

Network Isolation and Segmentation

Some organizations have been providing network isolation or segmentation for desktops for a long time now. This was done at the physical network layer, and primarily done for physical devices. The goal was to isolate these desktops or offer some level of control over what they can talk to in the data center.

Most large organizations will at minimum have a group of networks (VLANs) that are dedicated for end-user device connections. The next question is do they do anything to control the traffic between these end user networks and the networks in the data center? This is where organizations very greatly. There seems to be two common approaches to this question: the first being they do nothing. An end user on their laptop while in the office is allowed to reach nearly any IP address in the data center.

The other side of this coin is the organization has a firewall that isolates the end user networks from the data center networks. This approach can offer a greater degree of security, but taking too heavy of a locked down approach can create an environment that is incredibly difficult to manage.

Within the virtual desktop, hosted desktop, and hosted application space, using one or some of these physical network approaches can offer similar protection. Let's use a single virtual desktop use case as an example for this method. This use case will use virtual desktops as the main method of access and the use case will have a dedicated pool of VMs. This pool of virtual desktops will be configured to use a dedicated network created solely for this use case.

The sample use case has pretty minimal requirements within the data center. They will need to connect to the internet, the desktops will need to communicate with the VDI broker servers and there are just a couple of applications that they utilize that are all on a single network. This provides multiple options that one could take for these approaches.

The first would be to have all traffic entering or leaving the VDI VLAN for this use case to flow through a physical firewall device in the data center. This supports fine-grained control over what the design will allow these virtual desktops to communicate with. The design will be easily able to only grant them access to the internet, allow for the VDI brokers to establish connectivity, and allow for connections to the required application servers. All other traffic would be dropped by the firewalls.

Architecting EUC Solutions | 209

The scenario here would allow us to prevent traffic from Pool 1 to Pool 2 in both directions. It would be possible to allow traffic from Pool 1 to the entire App Servers network or to just specific application servers. The entire Services network would be accessible from Pool 1. All of the desktops within pool 1 would be able to communicate with each other. The internet would be accessed through the perimeter firewall. The following diagram illustrates a sample of this alternative.

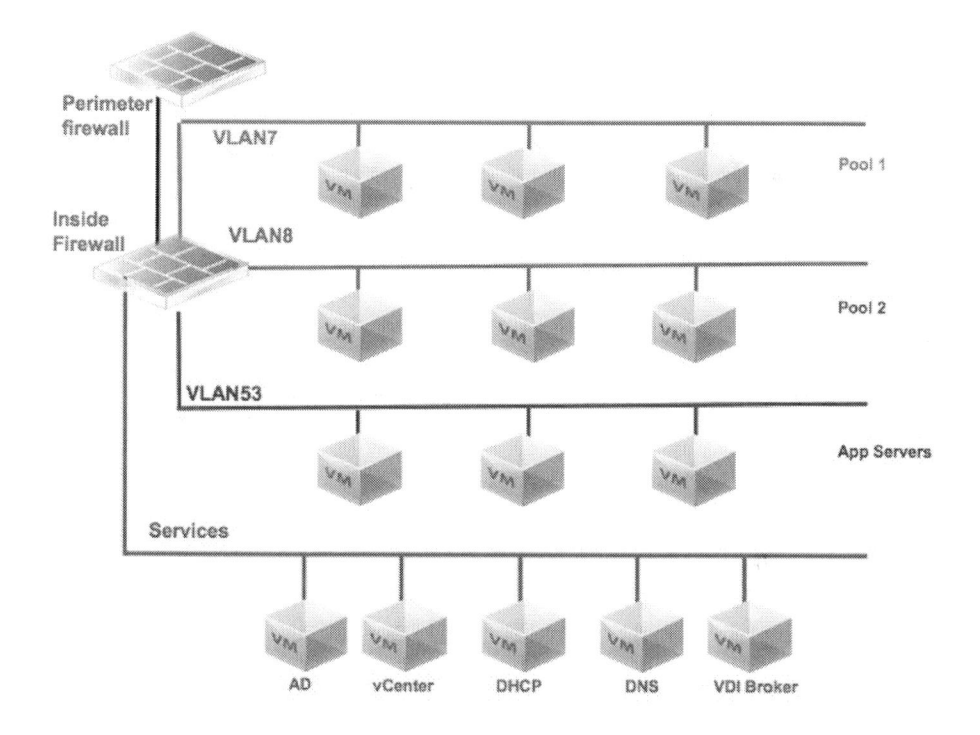

The second option for the sample use case would be to control the routing of traffic from the VDI VLAN. This provides less control because it is now dealing with only having control over whether to allow communication to another entire network versus with the firewall option having control at the IP address level.

With this alternative, you would be simply configuring routes leaving the VDI VLAN to the internet, to the entire network that application servers are on, and to the entire network that the VDI broker servers are on. This sort of accomplishes the goal, and is better than nothing. It still allows pretty wide access within the data center, though.

This scenario here would allow one to prevent traffic from Pool 1 to Pool 2 in both directions. It would allow traffic from Pool 1 to the entire App Servers network and to the entire Services network, as well through the perimeter firewall out to the internet. You would do this by only configuring routes to the networks selected to allow communication to. All of the desktops within Pool 1 would be able to communicate with each other. The following diagram illustrates a sample of this alternative.

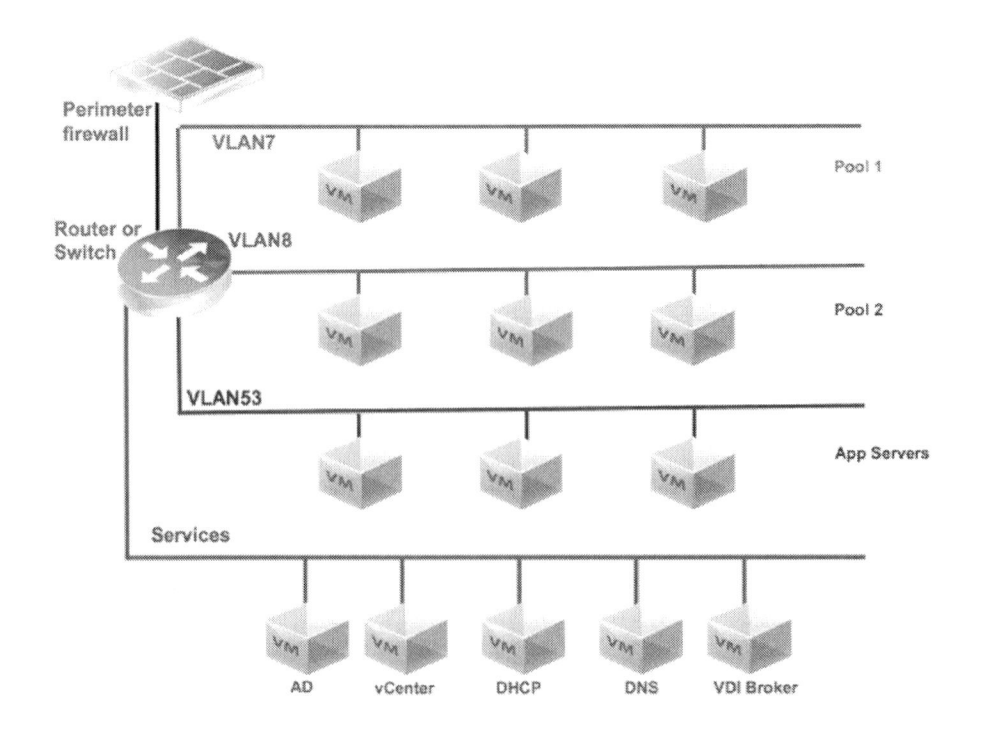

Micro Segmentation

The idea of micro segmentation has been getting a lot of attention recently. In the past, designs created large pools of virtual desktops that existed on a single network or on a few networks. The desktops on the same network were allowed to freely communicate with each other, and in some instances they are allowed to communicate with desktops on other networks. This approach opens up the ability for someone to gain access to another desktop, and perform malicious tasks or steal data.

This open approach also plans into the spread of viruses mentioned earlier in this chapter. Micro segmentation use a virtual firewalls to protect each virtual desktop from each other. The firewall rules would typically prevent Layer 2 communications between the local desktops, unless there was a requirement for this. There would be firewall rules that would allow communications to applications, user data, and other centrally located services.

VMware NSX allows this to be easily accomplished through the use of software based firewalls in the virtualization layer. This could also be accomplished through guest-based firewalls that are installed in each OS. Although the latter approach would be more difficult to deploy and manage, it is an option.

While gathering the requirements of each of your use cases, you can determine whether this is a feature that you will need to account for in your design. There are a number of common use cases that can benefit from this networking approach. Use cases such as external vendors, contract workers or offshore workers are all prime choices for this type of network isolation.

In this alternative NSX allows control at a per-VM basis to control traffic to and from any address. You can easily prevent traffic from individual Pool 1 desktops to Pool 2 desktops in both directions. You can also on a per-VM or user basis allow traffic from Pool 1 to the App Servers network and to the Services network, as well through the perimeter firewall out to the internet. The following diagram illustrates a sample of this alternative.

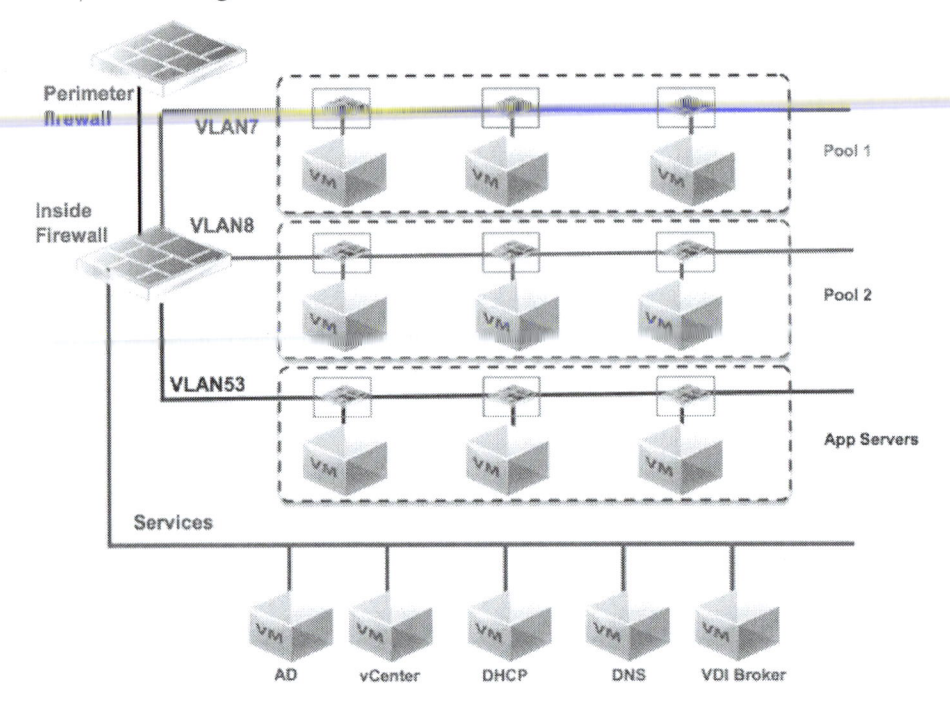

Summary

There are a number of security related topics when it comes to EUC designs. Typically, these are focused on access to services and data from internal and external locations. With increasing sensitivity around data breaches and privacy regulations, the inter-use securities covered in this chapter's examples are quickly becoming a hotter topic of discussion.

[17]
Endpoints

The endpoint is the device that your users interact with when they are consuming the EUC services. It will also be the device with which they have a good or bad experience. If the graphics look bad or something is slow they will likely look to blame the endpoint first. The endpoint is also something that can invoke a joyful experience when used or be like a knife that stabs them each time they use. Let's face it; end users are using some pretty cool technology every day in their personal lives. If they come to work and see a boring matte black box that sucks, they might just let you know about it. Most are not in the habit of buying shiny things just to please users, but you should look for a well-designed piece of gear that still meets the requirements.

Within if your EUC design, there will likely be the need for multiple endpoint options. You will have use cases that require only a single endpoint option, while others may need a few options. The endpoint decision for each use case will be driven by the use case's requirements, along with any environmental constraints. This chapter will educate on the types of endpoints, why they matter and offer some thoughts on how choices can be made.

Endpoint types

A majority of endpoints can be grouped into just a few categories that sum up their capabilities.

Rich Clients   Thin Clients   Mobile Clients

Rich Client - This category covers Desktop PCs and laptops that are running a full OS. This would include Windows, Linux, and MAC OS. They are also referred to as full clients, fat clients, or just PCs. These clients are perfectly suited to perform work on their own without any central EUC services, but also make a very powerful access point to centralized services. A rich endpoint allows for the option to allow all or part of the end users' functions to be performed on the device directly. Organizations may also leverage a rich endpoint for the access device when the user will do all their work in a centralized service. This could be for features provided by a rich device or simply a cost savings measure.

Thin Client - These days a thin client is a large category with many options and form factors in it. The hardware is generally a small footprint device that has little to no moving parts, which help thin clients last longer than other devices. The normal thin client option is still around and popular. There are also mobile thin clients which use a laptop form factor and there are all-in-one devices that embed the client into a flat screen monitor, as an example. Thin clients may or may not have an OS; typically this is broken down to zero clients or embedded devices. The zero clients do not run a typical OS, making them easy to manage and provides a very small security footprint to worry about. The embedded devices are running an embedded version of Windows or Linux typically that provides a look and feel closer to a full OS while limiting what can be done on the devices.

Mobile Client - The mobile category is pretty easy to define- mobile clients are either smartphones or tablets that are running a mobile OS. Although the line between a mobile OS and desktop OS is blurring as vendors are working on creating universal applications. The mobile clients are exclusively touch based devices, which must be taken into consideration, when evaluating the user experience.

Why Do They Matter?

There are a number of reasons why the type of endpoint matters in your design; they could be end user driven, environmentally driven, cost driven, performance, and feature driven. Your end users in one or all use cases may just want or require a set of features or form factor that is met by a specific type of endpoint. This will need to be heavily considered when making the endpoint selection for that use case. This is a delicate line to walk, as you want to be flexible and allow end-user input, but you do not want to be limited in your design choices by conceding to all the requests. On the flip side you cannot be too ridged, and not allow the end users input into some of these choices.

Other use cases may have strict environmental constraints that need to be considered when evaluating endpoint options. A constraint could be something as simple as limited amount of space. This could be as simple as altering your initial thin client choice to be a monitor with the thin client embedded, saving space in the end-user's work space. Other constraints may be more complex, such as a manufacturing environment. This could have harsher constraints, such as extreme dust, requirement to be blast proof, or a number of other strict requirements. These constraints will likely limit your endpoint choices and once you find your alternatives there will be little decision left.

Features

The feature set of the endpoint is probably the most determining factor when matching the right endpoints to each use case. As covered earlier Chapter 2, by this point one should fully understand the requirements of the use cases. These requirements will be factored into the endpoint selection process.

From the three types of endpoints that were explained, there are broads sets of the features are shared across each of the endpoint types. Each type of endpoint does offer some unique features and possibly performance benefits or sacrifice. Depending on the configuration, you should expect that a rich endpoint will typically be able to outperform the other endpoint options in scenarios where local resources are required or able to be utilized for a better experience. This is because the rich endpoint has a full featured CPU and likely more memory than the other endpoint types.

Within the thin client category there can be a very wide difference in configuration and performance. If you select a thin client on the higher end of the scale, it can often rival the performance that you would expect from a rich client. The decision then becomes a cost and management comparison. What would the pros and cons be between the two over the lifetime of the device?

They may be a peripheral or device that requires a full operating system or maybe only works on Windows; this may drive you to use a rich client or a thin client with embedded Windows as the OS. You would then need to evaluate which one you feel meets the minimum requirements and is easier to manage for the operations team. There has long been a debate about thin clients with embedded Windows, some organizations like them while others feel they are just as hard, or harder, to manage than rich clients.

Outside of performance and the other features discussed the connectivity will also be a point to consider. How many USB ports and other ports do each alternative offer and what network connectivity options do the options offer? If you intend on having all of your endpoints connect via wireless and your organization utilizes a certificate to join the network, will each of your endpoints support this. In the past there has been some challenges with this around the zero client devices, this could affect your decision if you favored zero clients as your thin client choice.

Mobility

The mobility of the endpoint can be driven by real requirements or just user preference. Being mobile does not exactly mean it needs to be a mobile device, the use case requirements may simple state that the user needs the ability to move between rooms or maybe someone that roams around during their workday. This many times translate that they still need a typical desktop device and a tablet with a touch interface will not meet their needs. The options for this could be a rich client in the form of a laptop, some vendors also offer a thin client that is packaged in a laptop form factor. These mobile thin clients look just like a laptop but have the inner workings of a thin client and are mobile, they have a battery to work disconnected. This allows the user to move around and you are able to still benefit from the operational benefits you desired from the thin client alternative.

Today there are multiple endpoint alternatives to allow your end users to work mobile, use the same evaluation process to select the right device to me the use cases requirements. End users may immediately request an iPad as the device because its what they use personally. If your applications are not mobile based or web based and optimized for touch interfaces then the user experience is going to suffer. This will be where a laptop or mobile thin client is going to excel and still allow the user to be mobile.

Access Clients

The access client is the software client that the EUC vendor offers for connectivity to their EUC services this. Historically this has been a software client that has been installed on the endpoint, a mobile application or come pre-installed on thin clients. In recent years the market is seeing the large EUC vendors support the ability to access their services through a web based client such as HTML5. This allows end users to access their applications and desktops through any HTML5 browser as an example.

While using an HTML session is very easy and convenient it may offer a reduced set of features and different experience to your users that you will need to consider. Depending on the vendors implementation of the web client there may be different limits, currently locally connected USB devices are not able to be passed back through to the virtual session as an example. Aside from a few limits the user experience has already proven to be great in these web clients. There is little to no difference in the performance of the session. The last thing to consider would be the user experience in the sense that they are accessing the application or virtual desktop in a browser tab. This feels a bit less than a native experience since you see the other browser tabs and all the menus from the browser at the top which results in less usable screen space. You have they option to work in full screen mode or kiosk mode for the browser but this would typically be a setting the end user would need to choose especially if its not a corporate owned device.

With the full access client software there can still be a differing set of features between the client on different operating systems. A vendor may offering client drive redirection on Windows devices but not on Mac OS or Linux devices. So even if you choose a rich client as the endpoint for a use case you will still need to carefully evaluate the features of the client for your vendor if the endpoint will not be a Windows only option. To this point all of the vendors have done a poor job of properly informing admins of all the features of their clients and which endpoints and operating systems they are available one. To get the full picture you will typically have to read entire client PDF manuals and do some Google searching.

Evaluating thin clients

A topic that comes up often with organizations is what is the best thin client or which one should they buy. The "It depends" consulting answer, definitely

Operating System

With thin clients there are really three primary operating system options available from vendors. They are zero clients, Windows embedded and Linux embedded, not all vendors will offer all of these options. When it comes to supporting and updating these OS alternatives they range from very easy on the zero client side to more time consuming on the Windows embedded side with Linux being some place in the middle. A Windows embedded device will still need to have Windows updates applied to it, so it will need to be updated far more than zero client or Linux versions. But the Windows embedded device may be able to provide features or work with peripherals that the others cannot. These are just a few of the things to consider in your thin client evaluations.

Display options

You build the best infrastructure in the data center the performs like a rock star, but if the remote user experience suffers you will have serious trouble. When evaluating thin clients you will want to take note of your display requirements based on use cases and your earlier design choices. Will you have use cases that require multiple monitors or have certain display resolution requirements? Another factor that can heavily affect your decision is do then thin clients being evaluated have any features that help with display performance such as Citrix HDX or PCoIP for VMware? These types of features allow for local resources to help with the intensive parts of the remote sessions allowing for a better user experience.

Management Options

Last up in the evaluation discussion would be the management of these thin devices. If you are going to be deploying hundreds or thousands of these devices the operation management of these devices and updates should be factored into your decision. If two devices from different vendors offer the same user experience but one has a far superior management offering that would heavily affect the decision.

The main things to consider around management would be around the deployment and updates of devices. Is there a tool or process that makes these functions easy to perform and achieve at your scale? Are there options around configuring policy and device management within the tool? The ability to report of settings and versions is very important so that you can ensure that devices are running the right versions and allow you to audit settings. Some organizations may also be required to collect inventory data from these devices, if the management tool is able to offer this also can be a helpful feature.

Decision tree sample

Once you have evaluated the requirements from all of your use cases and have selected a single endpoint per use case or have some that might have multiple options, an endpoint decision tree maybe helpful. This can be a simple flowchart that based on the answers to the questions guides you to the proper endpoint for the user or use case. These decision trees can be helpful for engineers and admins once the design has been deployed or may have a version that is published for business leaders to help understand what endpoint to request when on boarding new users.

The following is a simple example of an endpoint decision tree that you can use as a start for your project. If you have a complex environment you may have a high level tree that sends you to subordinate trees or just create one really large one.

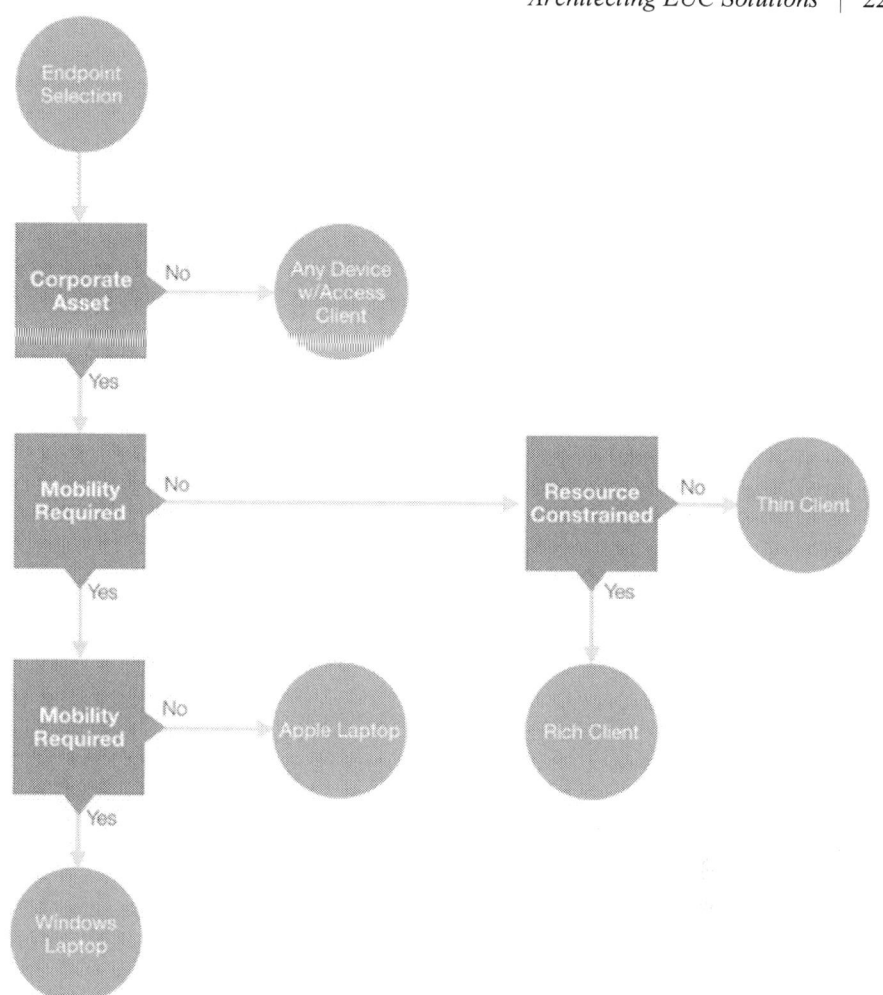

Summary

To summarize what was discussed in this chapter the endpoints can greatly affect the user experience in both the quality of their experience and how they feel about the device. Today more than ever, end users are connected to their devices and your design should try to avoid them from having the feeling of using some ancient device that work forces them to use.

[A]
Appendix – Nutanix Design Example

As a sample design scenario this example will walk through the design and sizing steps for a 2000 seat virtual desktop environment running on Nutanix infrastructure. This sample is simply one or two of the many possible alternatives, but can be used for guidance in real world designs. Nutanix was selected for the example, but the CPU and Memory portion of the example applies to all Intel based servers. The storage portion would be different based on the solutions you are evaluating.

The example scenario will have the following requirements.

- 1700 virtual desktops that require 1 vCPU and 2 GB of memory each, 250MHz CPU usage
- 300 virtual desktops that require 2 vCPU and 4 GB of memory each, 380 MHz CPU usable
- Management cluster is large enough to utilize 4 hosts
- No more than 14:1 ratio for 1 vCPU VMs
- No more than 6:1 ratio for 2 vCPU VMs

Too keep things simple, a Nutanix model and configuration has been pre-selected to make this example easier. The example will use Nutanix NX-3060-

G4 nodes with 12 core CPUs and 512 GB of memory. The following tables will break down the configuration according to the design topics discussed earlier.

The first table below is summarizing the CPU configuration of the nodes that will be used. The nodes are dual socket hosts with 12 cores per CPU. For this exercise the goal is to target a maximum of 80% CPU utilization, so the example has figured that as the available capacity. This is a number a lot of customers feel comfortable with, but using into the low 90 percentile after an HA event should be the ultimate goal.

ATTRIBUTE	VALUE
Sockets per host	2
Cores per CPU	12
MHz per Core	2,500 MHz
Total MHz per CPU	30,000 MHz
Total MHz per host	60,000 MHz
CPU utilization max	80%
Available MHz per host	48,000 MHz

The following table is similar to the previous CPU details, but focused on the memory of each node. The example is again targeting no more than 80% utilization under normal conditions. The calculations have also included the Nutanix controller VM (CVM) memory in this table to account for the memory that will be consumed outside of the virtual desktops. The 80% example here again is conservative and you should seek to use all available resources possible.

ATTRIBUTE	VALUE
Total RAM per host	512 GB
RAM utilization max	80%
Available RAM per host	409 GB
Nutanix CVM RAM	32 GB
Available RAM per host	377 GB

The 32GB of memory consumed by the Nutanix Controller VM (CVM) is the worst case, with every possible feature turned on. In VDI environments the CVM memory can range between 16-32GB depending on requirements.

Single vCPU Desktops

The first calculation in the example here will be for the larger pool, that has 1700 desktops with 1 vCPU each. The following table shows the calculations that were performed based on the previous host sizing and the desired to not exceed 80% utilization. Those values were used in the following calculations.

ATTRIBUTE	VALUE	NOTES
Desktop Count	1,700	
Total vCPU	1,700	1vCPU per VM
Total RAM	3,400 GB	2GB per VM
Total CPU	425,000 MHz	250MHz per VM
Target CPU Consolidation	14:1	vCPU:pCPU
Physical CPU Cores needed	1700/14 = 121 cores	Total vCPU/CPU Ratio = Total number of pCPU cores needed
Nodes needed per CPU	121/24 = 5.04 nodes	24 Cores per node
Nodes needed per RAM	3400GB/377GB = 9 nodes	377GB per node
Nodes need per CPU speed	425,000/48,000 = 8.8 nodes	48,000 MHz per node

Depending on which value you look at, the numbers show different requirements for the number of nodes. The CPU cores are the least restrictive, and only require just over five (5) nodes. While the RAM and CPU speed calculations show that the example will need nine (9) nodes. The final cluster size for this group of desktops will be 10 nodes. This will include the nine (9) nodes required for resources, and a 10th node for vSphere high availability protection.

In the end, the example did not reach the 14:1 CPU consolidation set as a goal, because the CPU speed and RAM were constraining factors in the sizing. This is fine, and most customers will have no objections either. The nodes that were chosen had a max memory of 512 GB. You could have chosen a different model with a higher memory configuration and saved a few hosts.

> *It does not matter the server vendor this applies to all that use Intel CPUs. You do not want to go past 512GB of memory in each server as it will lower the memory speed and reduce performance by 20-30%.*

As newer versions of Windows keep increasing their demand on memory and the average desktop VM now has 2-4GB of memory, we will continue to see host memory as the constraining value when sizing nodes. Most will find this to be a good balance and is not too aggressive for normal admins.

The 10 hosts needed for this use case is large enough to warrant its own hypervisor cluster. We could certainly combine the two different desktop use cases into a single cluster, it would make the math a bit more interesting with different VM CPU sizes. But assuming that each of these use cases will grow, the desire to have a discrete cluster for each will make sizing and management easier over time.

Dual vCPU Desktops

The second calculation in the example here will be for the smaller pool that has 300 desktops with two vCPU each. The following table shows the calculations that were performed based on the previous host sizing and the desired to not exceed 80% utilization. Those values were used in the following calculations.

ATTRIBUTE	VALUE	NOTES
Desktop Count	300	
Total vCPU	600	2vCPU per VM
Total RAM	1,200 GB	4GB per VM
Total CPU	114,000 MHz	380MHz per VM
Target CPU Consolidation	6:1	vCPU:pCPU
Physical CPU Cores needed	600/6 = 100 cores	Total vCPU/CPU Ratio = Total number of pCPU cores needed
Nodes needed per CPU	100/24 = 4.16 nodes	24 Cores per node
Nodes needed per RAM	1200GB/377GB = 3.18 nodes	377GB per node
Nodes need per CPU speed	114,000/48,000 = 2.3 nodes	48,000 MHz per node

For the two vCPU group of virtual desktops the same calculations were made, the main difference is that due to the additional vCPUs the example will be using a lower consolidation ratio. The nodes needed to satisfy CPU core requirements was just a bit over four (4) nodes. If you were feeling aggressive, you could round down. You should play it safe, though, and round up if it is more than 10% of the next node.

In this case the numbers. say it need five nodes to meet the resource requirements. A sixth node will be added for vSphere high availability. By rounding up, it also provides some room for growth before needing to add another node.

In this example where the use case had more vCPUs and a lower consolidation ratio the CPU calculation was the limiting factor. Depending on the use case requirements, 6:1 CPU ratio may be a bit low and you may be able to achieve better density with a higher ratio.

The decision here is also to use a dedicate hypervisor cluster for this use case as we have six hosts to start. We could combine with the previous example and be starting with a 16 node cluster which is perfectly acceptable. This example customer expects to grow this environment that along with the different CPU configurations is plenty of justification for the different clusters.

On the other side if this design had no expectation of growth or if the numbers where smaller it would be a recommendation to consider a single cluster.

Management Cluster

I have not provided the sizing calculations for the management cluster in this example in effort to keep things simple. The main focus was around sizing for desktop workloads. The management cluster would be running the two vCenter servers- one for management and one for desktops. It will also be running monitoring tools, file servers, Citrix or VMware VDI brokers, as well as the application servers (RDSH or XenApp).

These server-based VMs require the resources from four (4) Nutanix 3060 nodes configured with 12 core CPUs and 256 GB of memory. A fifth node will be added to the cluster for vSphere high availability protection.

The option was presented in the desktop clusters to separate or combine into a single cluster. The management cluster in any design unless very small should be separate from the desktops. This is done for both the separation of management from workloads and also because they are both very different workloads. Depending on available resources and funding you may elect to build a new management cluster as we did in this example or co-locate these VMs with existing server VMs if you have available resources in your existing environment.

Nutanix Storage Cluster Alternatives

The examples in this chapter have just taken a look at how the vSphere clusters would be sized. There will be a total of three clusters to accommodate the management resources and the two desktop groups. At the Nutanix storage cluster level, there are several options that can be looked at. There are three alternatives that will be expanded on below and explain the pros and cons of each. This is a design decision that you should weigh your availability requirements against and use with all factors to make any decisions.

Three Storage Cluster

This first alternative has created discrete Nutanix storage clusters that match the vSphere clusters that were created earlier in the example design. It has made sure that each cluster would have enough storage capacity to fulfill the VM requirements and the data protection requirements. This approach has its pros and cons like any alternative design choice does, each has been elaborated on below.

For this scenario we are assuming that each cluster would be configured for Replication Factor of 3 (RF3), which allows each storage cluster to sustain two node failures simultaneously. This provides a higher level of redundancy, but requires at least 5 nodes in a cluster to enable. Since each of the example clusters fit that requirement and also still fit within the usable capacity of the cluster it was chosen.

Pros

- Isolated failure domains - Each cluster can sustain a double failure allowing for a greater total number of failures within the design.
- No additional nodes were required to meet this alternative.

Cons

- The Isolated failure domains do not allow each cluster to take advantage of global capacity and performance benefits.

While this alternative does create three different failure domains, it also divides up the global resources in doing so. This would not affect our performance required for this solution and is considered acceptable as the design is expected to grow over time. If the environment was not expected to grow from this point having fewer failure domains as explained in the following alternatives may be more appealing.

Cluster Protection

The Replication Factor (RF) will be set to RF3 for each Nutanix cluster. Allowing a double failure in each cluster.

Failure Domain

The failure domains have been limited to the boundaries of each vSphere and Nutanix cluster.

- Mgmt Cluster Nutanix #1
- Desktop Cluster 1 Nutanix #2
- Desktop Cluster 2 Nutanix #3

Two Storage Clusters

This second alternative has created just two Nutanix storage clusters, one for management and one for desktop resources. It has made sure that each cluster would have enough storage capacity to fulfill the VM requirements and the data protection requirements. This approach has its pros and cons, just as any alternative design choice does, and they are elaborated on below.

This alternative also uses an RF3 level to protect against a dual failure within each of the clusters.

Pros

- Semi-Isolated failure domains - The management and collapsed desktop clusters can each sustain a double failure allowing for a greater total number of failures within the design.
- No additional nodes were required to meet this alternative.

Cons

- The isolated failure domains do not allow each cluster to take advantage of global capacity and performance benefits.
- The entire desktop storage pool can only sustain a double node failure.

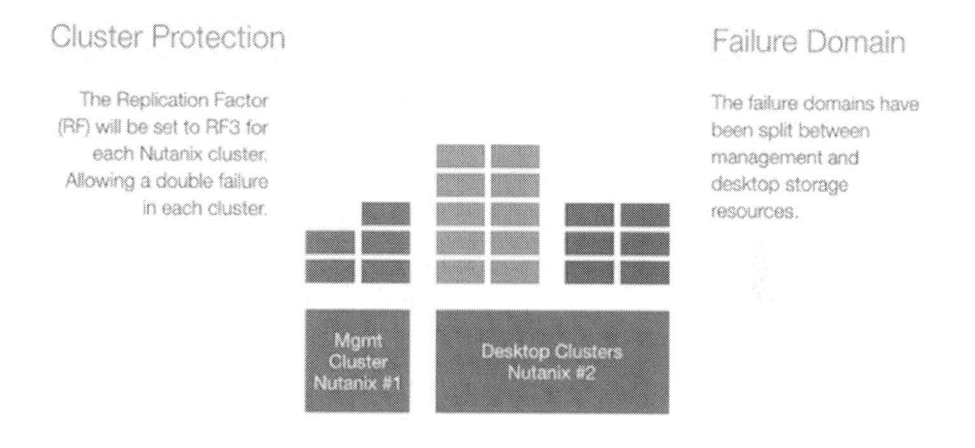

Cluster Protection

The Replication Factor (RF) will be set to RF3 for each Nutanix cluster. Allowing a double failure in each cluster.

Failure Domain

The failure domains have been split between management and desktop storage resources.

Mgmt Cluster Nutanix #1

Desktop Clusters Nutanix #2

In this example we have collapse the desktop failure domain, but are still protected against a dual failure. Since the hypervisor clusters were large enough we were able to accomplish this without the need for any additional hosts. Taking this collapsed approach by combining resources can allow multiple smaller clusters to benefit from the higher RF levels by combining resources.

Single Storage Cluster

This last alternative has created a single Nutanix storage cluster for all of the vSphere clusters, identified earlier in the example design. It has made sure that the cluster would have enough storage capacity to fulfill the VM requirements and the data protection requirements. This approach has its pros and cons, just as any alternative design choice does. They are elaborated on below.

Pros

- The single failure domain allows each of the vSphere clusters to take advantage of global capacity and performance benefits of the greater Nutanix storage cluster.
- No additional nodes were required to meet this alternative.

Cons

- Singe failure domain - All of the resources are now collapsed into a single failure domain, which can sustain a double failure.
- This did not reduce the number of nodes in the design.

Cluster Protection

The Replication Factor (RF) will be set to RF3 for the Nutanix cluster. Allowing a double failure in the cluster.

Failure Domain

A single failure domain have been split between that contains the management and desktop storage resources.

Management & Desktop Clusters
Nutanix Cluster

This last alternative shows how we have moved from multiple storage clusters to a single. The decision of which approach is right for your design will be tied to your requirements and desire to control the size of your failure domains.

It makes perfect sense if you will have multiple small clusters to combine them to allow for the option to use a higher RF protection level, but also take advantage of the greater pool of capacity and performance resources. This decision is also influenced by the starting and expected maximum size of your environment. If are starting small but know you will scale to a larger size then multiple clusters probably makes sense. If you are unsure then you could start combined with a plan on how you would scale into multiple clusters as the environment grows.

Summary

This design and sizing example for Nutanix is intended to provide a thought process on the different alternatives to consider when designing for your project. Sizing was intentionally somewhat conservative to protect architects with lesser amounts of EUC and HCI experience. Once you have a first pass of your design created this is an excellent opportunity to socialize it with someone from Nutanix to provide feedback and answer any questions.

Nutanix has created a sizer for this specific purpose that includes pre-defined workload sizes for EUC, server VMs, databases, and other important business applications. The sizer combines years of application and design experience to confirm your sizing choices or provide a beginning point for others. The sizer is available to Nutanix employees, OEM partners and channel partners for you to work with.

Index

antivirus, 205
app store, 127
application inventory, 50
assessment, 43, 44
Assumptions, 2, 4
backup, 145, 169
bandwidth, 154, 155, 156
baseline, 49
building block, 181
BYO, 183
BYOD, 73, 92
capacity, 135, 179
compute, 195
conceptual design, 29
Concurrency, 17
Constraints, 2, 4
converged infrastructure, 185, 187
DaaS, 81, 84, 85, 86, 87
Dedicated, 68
DHCP, 151
disaster recovery, 122, 133
Endpoint, 17, 77, 215, 222
EUC, 91, 126
evaluation, 8
failover, 135, 143
firewall, 159
folder redirection, 121
full clone, 59
GPO, 100
GPU, 16, 70
hyperconverged, 188, 189, 190
infrastructure, 175
IOPS, 48, 191
KMS, 98
latency, 152, 153
layering, 106, 107
Linked clones, 61, 62, 64, 101
load balancer, 158
logical design, 30
MCS, 61, 62, 69, 101, 192
Mirage, 76

monitoring, 164, 165, 180
network, 147, 148, 169
non-persistent, 54, 58, 59, 60, 64, 67, 145
NVIDIA GRID, 71
Objectives, 4
PCLM, 94
performance, 178
persistent, 54, 55, 57, 58, 64, 112, 140, 145
physical design, 31
Pilot, 35, 39
POC, 35, 39
pooled, 68
portal, 125
profile, 115, 120, 122
PVS, 65, 69, 101, 150, 192
RDSH, 68, 70, 104
replication, 137, 142
reporting, 162
requirements, 2, 13, 16, 24
Risks, 2, 4
roadmap, 9, 11, 23
runbook, 138
scalability, 177
SCCM, 74, 94, 101, 107
security, 159, 201
Shared Hosted, 68
skills, 166, 172
SLAs, 84
SSL, 207
SSO, 126, 203
storage, 190
team, 166, 170, 171
thin client, 216, 221
Two-factor, 203
UEM, 115, 117
use case, 15
use cases, 13, 18, 41, 77
vCPU, 197

VDI, 55, 56, 60, 69, 79, 82, 112, 115, 148, 157, 192
vendor selection, 7

vGPU, 78
writable volumes, 113

Printed in Great
Britain
by Amazon